THE 21 LAWS OF EVANGELISM

By Jack Redmond

Jack Redmond

Matt 28: 19 - 20

THE 21 LAWS OF EVANGELISM

*Biblical Principles Guaranteed to
Turn the World Upside Down*

JACK REDMOND

The 21 Laws of Evangelism

Biblical Principles Guaranteed to Turn the World Upside Down

Copyright © 2017—Jack Redmond

www.jackredmond.org

COVER AND INTERIOR LAYOUT: SWINGHOUSE DESIGN STUDIOS
ISBN-13: 9780692977415 / ISBN-10: 0692977414
PRINTED IN THE UNITED STATES OF AMERICA.

This book is dedicated to my father, John William Redmond II. He was a faithful family man, he loved his country, had great strength and was a man of quiet faith and few words. He spent his life making the world a better place.

He passed away unexpectedly on June 5, 2016. I spent the next 21 days writing a chapter a day of **The 21 Laws of Evangelism**. I wrote to help me process the loss and to honor my father who gave so much to so many.

He married his high school sweetheart Loretta, and they were married for 49 years. He coached my Little League team and we played catch many times. He took me fishing every weekend for a whole summer and we never even caught a fish! He didn't know how to fish, but for some reason, I was a kid who wanted to go, so he took me every Saturday. To this day, one of my favorite things to do is to fish. He worked harder than any man I know and never really wanted anything or asked for anything from anyone. He gave.

My prayer is that the impact of his life continues through my life and this book.

He helped me gain a love for catching fish. I pray this book gives people a love for winning souls.

Dad, I miss you and I pray that this book honors you and will result in many people spending eternity with us in heaven.

Love, your son,
John William Redmond III

CONTENTS

INTRODUCTION

*If sinners be damned, at least let them leap to Hell over our dead bodies.
And if they perish, let them perish with our arms wrapped about their knees,
imploring them to stay. If Hell must be filled, let it be filled in the teeth of our
exertions, and let not one go unwarned and unprayed for.*[1]

–CHARLES SPURGEON

Many types of laws exist: natural laws, physical laws, man-made laws, and also spiritual laws. Natural and spiritual laws have existed since time began and merely await our discovery. In contrast, man-made laws are created over time to promote order and even control of society.

This book focuses on spiritual laws, and we will look to the Bible for explanation and understanding. As you will soon discover, spiritual laws come with consequences—both good and bad. Ultimately, these consequences are designed to steer us toward the best way to live.

In *The Twenty-One Laws of Evangelism*, we focus specifically on God's plan for man to know Him, both now and for eternity. The laws set forth in His Word give us a roadmap, instructing us on how to interact with God and others. When we follow these laws, we can help those disconnected from God learn to connect with Him, both now and for eternity.

Yes, this is amazing news; we get to partner with God as we point others to Him. The other option is horrible. When people connect with Jesus, heaven is the result. Without coming to know Him, the only other option for these souls is to spend eternity separated from God in a place called hell.

Many people shy away from speaking about hell; others use the word and concept to scare. We must neither shy away from this difficult topic nor use it to manipulate people. The reality is that we are eternal beings who will spend eternity either with God in heaven or separated from God in hell. Ignoring this reality will not change it.

The goal of *The Twenty-One Laws of Evangelism* is to help you help others connect with Jesus. Each chapter will clearly explain God's plan and your part in that plan.

Every day, you encounter people who are disconnected from God. If this sobering reality doesn't bother you, your heart has grown numb. Or maybe your heart is fearful and you are apprehensive to share your faith and God's love. Neither of these mindsets is God's will.

Each chapter details one spiritual law that is true of God's order and plan. As you read each law, God will open your heart and mind to understand His plan more clearly. Heaven is forever, and God wants to use you to connect others with Him. Get ready for God to do above and beyond what you have ever thought or imagined by the power that is already within you (Eph. 3:20).

Laws can provide clarity and order, creating peace by establishing cultural expectations and norms. They are useful when they guide behavior and prevent tragedy. Natural laws give our world a sense of predictability and order. If you drop something, it falls and increases in speed at a rate of 9.8 meters per second every second or 9.8 m/s/s.[2] This is the law of gravity.

Similarly, these twenty-one laws of evangelism explain God's predictable hand in the spread of the gospel. God is at work, and these laws explain how we can partner with Him to guide people to a personal relationship with Jesus. I am describing these scriptures and principles as "laws," meaning we can depend on them as fact. When we understand and trust these laws, our faith and personal confidence will grow. We will trust God's plans and expect Him to use us to win souls.

Winning souls is not just the job of the pastor, preacher, or evangelist; it is the job of every Christian. To believe anything else would demonstrate a lack of knowledge and understanding of God's Word. Over the centuries, a church culture has developed, especially in America and Europe, that relegates soul winning to a few specialists. Just as Jesus trained twelve "nobodies" to win souls, God continues this work today through people like you and me.

Thank you for taking this journey with me. I am trusting God to use us as we partner with Him to add souls to heaven.

SECTION 1

GOD'S PLAN: HEAVEN FULL

LAW

It is God's Will for
Every Person to Go to Heaven

The Lord is not slow in keeping His promise, as some understand slowness. Instead He is patient with you, not wanting anyone to perish, but everyone to come to repentance.

—2 PETER 3:9

This is good, and pleases God our Savior, who wants all people to be saved and to come to a knowledge of the truth.

—1 TIMOTHY 2:4

KEY TRUTH

It is God's will that every person makes it to heaven.

This is the foundational truth for our efforts. It removes any doubt about whether we should share our faith journey and the story of God's love. God gives people free choice to either accept or reject Him, and we can't control that. We can only control what *we* do. Our job is to do everything we can with every person we know to help them understand the gospel, the good news that God wants everyone to have a personal relationship with Him.

The Eternal Family Reunion

Think of the great lengths families go to when organizing a family reunion with their extended relatives. The organizers put extreme effort into contacting people and making sure everyone can make the reunion. They plan the food and entertainment. Some even make t-shirts printed, for example, with "Johnson Family Reunion 2017."

However extensive and impressive these efforts are here on earth, they pale in comparison to God's effort and desire to fill heaven with His children. The greatest family reunion we ever experience will be an eternal one in heaven. Throughout this book, we will look at God's will, plans, and effort to make sure everyone knows He wants them at this reunion.

We will also look at our role in this plan. Before a family reunion, the coordinators reach out to distant cousins, those disconnected from the family, and maybe even the black sheep who has caused shame. Similarly, God sends us to reach out to all people. Remember, healing and wholeness come when people reconnect with His family. The body of Christ can then nourish, encourage, and walk with new family members along life's path.

All Are Welcome!

Heaven is for everyone, not just the "special" or "good." In fact, outside of God's intervention, none of us are good. Despite our flaws, God loves each of us unwaveringly. He wants us to know Him and live in that love.

We are all created in God's image by Him and for Him.

Yet, when you woke up this morning, there were between five and six billion people disconnected from Jesus. This reality must break God's heart. It is not His will that anyone be separated from Him for one minute, never mind for all eternity.

Consider the first day of school. Every kindergarten teacher I know looks at the beautiful faces of her children on the first day of school and dreams that one day they will do great things. Teachers imagine these little ones becoming artists, lawyers, doctors, or maybe engineers. They don't wish for any to end up broken people, poorly educated or failures. If teachers have this passion and concern for children they are just meeting, imagine how God looks at the children He created. I use the word "children" loosely here and will later discuss the term "child of God" at length in chapter 12; please allow me some flexibility with the term here.

The love a teacher has pales in comparison to the love of God. The effort teachers exert also pale in comparison to the love and sacrifice of God the Father who sent His Son to die on the cross.

Now and for Eternity

Every time you look at someone, you can be confident it is God's will for them to have a relationship with Christ, both now and for eternity. The scriptures from 2 Peter and 1 Timothy at the beginning of this chapter clearly state God's will is that none "perish" but all come to a "saving knowledge" of Christ.

"Perish" means to be permanently disconnected from God, with no hope of reunion. This is never God's will. Rather, He deeply desires that all turn from sin and receive forgiveness and everlasting life. When man could not reach up to God, God came to earth in the form of man so that Jesus could be a bridge to the Father.

"Saving knowledge" means people come to understand how God works in a way that leads to eternal life. People must accept that each of us has sinned and is, therefore, separated from God. The only way to reconnect with God is to receive His forgiveness and put faith in Jesus' blood as a literal payment for sin. Forgiveness is truly a gift from God (Eph. 2:8-9). It is His will that every person learns these things and reconnects with Him.

The Foundational Law

I chose to make this law—it is God's will for every person to go to heaven—first because it enables us to see the other laws clearly. Each day we have feelings and emotions toward everyone we meet. For many reasons, it is easy to become frustrated or judgmental. Knowing God's will for every person can change the way we look at those we encounter. Instead of becoming annoyed, the truth of this law can encourage us to engage. Instead of avoiding the people we find harder to love, we can see our duty is to help them connect with God.

We will be less judgmental when we understand it is people's brokenness and disconnection with God that makes them act as they do. We can view them through the lens of the Father's love and redemptive plan, overlooking who they currently are.

We Are All Needed

As we consider the vast number of disconnected people, it is clear that the number of professional pastors and evangelists is insufficient to reach every soul. We understand it will take *all* who call Jesus "Lord" to reach the multitudes who don't yet know Him as Savior.

If Jesus is our Lord, we are to do His will, and His will is that none shall perish but all come to a saving knowledge of Him. If this is our Lord's will, it is to be our life's work. Few of us will ever be in full-time ministry as a vocation, but we are all called to ministry as followers of Christ. In God's view, no "professional" Christian designation exists; *all* of His Children are called to do His will, and that includes soul winning. Everywhere we go, we are on duty to help others connect with Jesus. We will continue to explore this concept throughout the book.

See People As He Sees Them

Bob Pierce was an evangelist who went to China to share the gospel and win souls for Christ. Along the way, he became a champion not only of feeding people spiritually but also of feeding hungry people physically, especially small children. I believe God wants us to do both. When we feed people physically, we help them in the present. When we feed them spiritually, we help them in the present and for all eternity. By knowing God's will and having God's heart, we start to live differently.

Pierce once said, "Let my heart be broken by the things that break the heart of God."[3] If you have the courage to pray to help win souls, get ready. God will start to change the way you look at people. Their brokenness will lead you to sorrow, not anger. You won't look at them with scorn, as some might look at a disobedient or obnoxious child. Rather, you will look at them as a parent, who more than anything wants her child to go the right way.

Sharing the Solution

When I gave my life to Christ at twenty-seven, one of the first things I realized was that peace with God was what I had been looking for and what everyone else was looking for, too. I quickly understood that if God gave me new life, He would do the same for others. So, I set out almost immediately to help others connect with Jesus.

I personally spent years looking for "it," the thing that would make me happy and content by filling my insatiable emptiness and hunger. Maybe you know the discontent I am describing. Maybe you are still searching. If you are a follower of Christ and have received the new life Jesus promised, your search is over. You have the solution others are looking for.

People are longing for the peace only God can give, the joy that brings strength, and the abundant life Jesus promised. Without Jesus, they cannot find these things; instead, they search for fulfillment through alcohol, relationships, and sin. This was my story, but after twenty-seven years of being disconnected from God, I discovered it was His will that I should know Him.

Each day, you have the chance to encourage others to take a step closer to connecting with Jesus in a life-changing way. Knowing God's plans are for everyone, we can have confidence when we talk to others about God.

We don't have to ask, "Who should I share my faith with?" We shouldn't look for some perfect when or where. Instead, we should be ready to share our story and the gospel anywhere, anytime, with anyone.

Action Steps

Read: 2 Peter 3:8-13

Reflection: Reflect and/or journal on God's Will for all men to be saved and have a personal relationship with Him. How does that affect how you look at people?

Action/Conversation:

1. Make a list of people who are disconnected from Jesus and pray each day that they will come to know Jesus as Lord and Savior.

2. Reach out to the people on your list. Speak to and spend time with them so that you have the opportunity to share your faith journey and the Gospel.

LAW

God Loves Everyone

For God so loved the world that he gave his one and only Son, that whoever believes in him shall not perish but have eternal life.

–JOHN 3:16

God is love.

–1 JOHN 1:4:8B

KEY TRUTH

God loves every single person—period!

God loves *everyone*. Period. End of story. Another way to say this is, God's love is unconditional, freely given to all, and not based on merit. When we embrace this biblical principle, our view of others will change. When people act in unlovely ways or we feel annoyed, we can be driven to love them anyway, compelled by God's love.

Love must become the lens through which we look and the end goal of our interactions with all people. Love can enable us to see the best in people, to want to help them overcome areas of brokenness. The law of love can remove barriers and soften our judgmental opinions. We are called to love all people and the greatest act of love is showing them Jesus.

Temporary vs. Eternal Needs

Over the years, when volunteering as a chaperone or watching my friends' children, I have felt a tremendous responsibility to be even more diligent than when watching my own children. At these times, I felt the weight and responsibility of caring for and protecting my precious charges. I personally owned the responsibility for making sure they were well fed and cared for.

This thought process can help us when we look at people as God's children. How should we care for them, help them, feed them? From a theological view, you can say these people are disconnected from God and, therefore, not "His children," but our goal is to help them become His children. The Gospel of John speaks to this transformation: "Yet to all who did receive him, to those who believed in his name, he gave the right to become children of God—children born not of natural descent, nor of human decision or a husband's will, but born of God" (1:12-13).

Imagine you have a friend's child staying with you, and he is currently being rebellious against his parents. Would you refuse to care for him because you didn't agree with his actions or behaviors? I think the reality is, most of us would actually go out of our way to do everything we could to help him smooth things out with his parents. That effort toward reconciliation would be an expression of love toward our friend and the child. In the same way, we can express love toward people who are currently disconnected from God.

Other times, I have come in contact with children I don't know. I have been in youth houses, where teens are sent due to criminal activity. I have also been at soup kitchens, where beautiful but disheveled children come in with their family or even alone. I have spent time with orphans in India, some who smile and laugh and others who cry, wondering what tomorrow will bring. My heart goes out to these precious children, and I know this love comes from God.

If I am concerned about their temporary needs—matters of food, clothing, and relationship—how much more should I be focused on their eternal well-being? Many of these children have been victims of circumstances beyond their control. Many have been neglected or abused. Most of those who have been incarcerated had powerful forces that pushed them to get involved in activities that grew to be criminal over time. They have not enjoyed love, guidance, or correction along the way and now desperately need God's love. We are called to be ambassadors of His eternal love.

God's Love Is Serious

God did not send a mere book of philosophy or yet another prophet. He sent His Only Son to take on and pay for sin so all people could connect with Him. Those who have not yet turned to Jesus are spiritual orphans, but God is waiting for them. We must tell them that Jesus became the ransom to buy us back for the Father: "For even the Son of Man did not come to be served, but to serve, and to give his life as a ransom for many" (Mk. 10:45).

This verse from Mark makes clear that Jesus traded His life for the lives of many. Some may think it is reasonable to make such a sacrifice for the "good" people who love Jesus, but His plan is much greater than that. God's love is given to all—even when we are at our worst: "But God demonstrates his own love for us in this: While we were still sinners, Christ died for us" (Rom. 5:8).

The word "sinner" here does not mean someone who made a one-time mistake. It means someone who purposely chooses an ongoing lifestyle of sin. The Amplified Bible renders Romans 5:8 like this, "But God clearly shows *and* proves His own love for us." God did not wait for us to be nice or good. Instead, Jesus freely gave His life, knowing that some would receive His love, but many would reject it. Jesus gave His life anyway because His love was so great.

The truth of God's unconditional love contradicts the false belief that God is an angry God, looking to "get" sinners. The exact opposite is true. God sent Christ so He would not have to punish us for wrong. Jesus paid the bill for our wrongdoing—even before we racked up the debt.

Love Drives out Fear

When we understand the truth of God's love for *all* people, our faith can grow. We can rest our full confidence in the power of a love that reaches people like nothing else can. This love can break down barriers and build bridges. One of the greatest obstacles of people coming to God is the idea that they are not good enough.

Many have been told by religion and religious people that they are "bad" or that God wouldn't want someone like them. This mistaken message can create anger toward religion and God. It can also create a fear of punishment, but 1 John 4:18 has something to say about that: "There is no fear in love. But perfect love drives out fear, because fear has to do with punishment."

When people receive the truth that God loves them, they receive a love that drives out fear. Imagine a mouse in your kitchen. You would likely pick up a broom and chase that mouse out of the house. We can all imagine this funny scene as a petrified mouse runs for its life. Just as you "drive out" the mouse, God's love will drive out the fear of not measuring up or of being punished by God.

Fear can be paralyzing, but love and faith leads to freedom. Anxiety and depression are often caused by a fear of not being accepted, but God's love and acceptance are for all. In fact, God not only offers love, but He *is* love (1 John 1:4:8b). Just as a tree is made out of wood and a bone is made out of calcium, God literally consists of love. It's His nature, His character, and His essence.

No Shortage of God's Love

God is infinite and so is His love. He has an unlimited ability to share a maximum amount of love. So, when we share the gospel, we can be bold, confident, and courageous, knowing that God has more than enough love to give.

We cannot let our limited experiences and abilities taint our view of what God can accomplish. Consider this scenario: you are at lunch and want to pay for your friends' food also, but you are afraid you will not have enough cash. You fear your limited supply of money may run out. Do you apply this same line of thought to your service of others?

If we try to operate within our human ability and resources, we will grow tired, and serving people will drain us. In contrast, God never gets tired and never runs out of love. We must learn to lean on and serve out of that never-ending supply of love.

Tapping into God's Love

God's love is not just something we can receive for ourselves; it is also something we can express to others because we are made in His image: "So, God created mankind in his own image, in the image of God he created them; male and female he created them" (Gen. 1:27). "Created in His image" means we reflect who God is in His essence. Since God is love and He loved the world enough to give His one and only Son, we have the ability to love like He does and make any sacrifice necessary to help people connect with Him.

This is the reason we are called to pray, worship, and study the Word. These acts not only allow us to know about Him, but they also allow us to experience Him in a way that makes us more like Him, concerned for the things that concern Him. These disciplines enable us to walk in His love and His power as we strive to lead people to Him. We must let God's Word, our prayer life, and our worship define who we are and what we do.

In short, one of the greatest evangelism tools we have is simply loving people. Many people have the knowledge, understanding, and even the desire to lead people to Christ, but they lack love, which often short circuits their efforts. I have seen others with no theological training, just a few biblical principles and a whole lot of love, able to win many souls to Jesus.

Action Steps

Read: John 3:1-21

Reflection: Reflect and/or journal on God's love. What does God's love mean to you? What does it mean to the people you will share the gospel and your personal story with?

Action/Conversation:
1. Have a conversation with someone and tell him God loves them. Then smile and continue the conversation.

LAW

We Are Saved by Grace through Faith

For it is by grace you have been saved, through faith—and this is not from yourselves, it is the gift of God—not by works, so that no one can boast.

–Ephesians 2:8-9

KEY TRUTH

Salvation is a gift from God received through faith.

Many feel unworthy to know God personally or to one day go to heaven to be with Him. The reality is that we are all unworthy. We all need a savior to save us from the penalty of sin. Because many people feel excluded by their past mistakes, they don't try to understand the gospel or learn about forgiveness. They never realize forgiveness is a gift given through faith that cannot be earned or lost through our efforts or actions. Working your way into heaven simply cannot be done. Yes, we should do good works, but the way to heaven is through grace alone.

One of the greatest roadblocks for people coming into a personal relationship with Jesus is feeling dirty, shameful, or unworthy. Religion often reinforces the idea of a stern and vengeful God. This view leaves people either scared of or mad at God. Misunderstandings about grace can build a

29

wall that keeps people from receiving God.

Saved by Grace through Faith

Grace is the opposite of punishment. In fact, one of the ways to define grace is God's unmerited favor. Grace is God's blessing for people who could never earn it. Being saved by grace means being forgiven of our sins and welcomed into relationship with Jesus, with no personal payment to make or just punishment to receive. People often wonder, then, how do we receive this grace?

We receive grace through faith as a gift from God, which goes against the religious teachings of every religion outside of Christianity (and even certain groups within Christianity). When people understand the reality of grace, they understand they are not accepted or rejected based on performance and can instead put their faith in the work of the cross.

Romans 10:9 describes the beautiful simplicity of salvation by grace through faith: "If you declare with your mouth, 'Jesus is Lord,' and believe in your heart that God raised him from the dead, you will be saved." Confessing with your mouth the truth you believe in your heart is the doorway to receiving God's forgiveness and grace.

Overcoming Pride

One of the keys to receiving grace is humility, and pride is one of the greatest obstacles to salvation through faith. Many feel they are "good people" and will not be judged for their sin. They point to other people, who are obviously "bad," and consider themselves superior, not in need of much help. They reason that a "good God" would never send "good people" to hell, so they are safe. Their moral deeds give them confidence that all will be well. In essence, they put their faith in their own goodness and, whether intentionally or not, set up a wall of pride between themselves and God.

Let's see what God's Word says in James 4:6 about proud and humble people: "But he gives all the more grace; therefore it says, 'God opposes the proud, but gives grace to the humble'" (NRSV). This truth makes clear that all must be humble to receive grace from God and moral comparisons do not ensure salvation.

A Gift from God

Because grace is received as a gift, those who feel unworthy can rest, knowing God's love and salvation is not about being good enough. Rather, forgiveness is a gift God wants to give freely. If someone buys you a gift, you don't have to pay for it or earn it; you simply receive it. This often seems too good for people to believe. But, yes, God is so generous that He is ready and willing to forgive people of every sin.

This gift of grace, though given for free through faith, is not cheap. Romans 6:23 tells us, "For the wages of sin is death, but the free gift of God is eternal life in Christ Jesus our Lord." The "wages," meaning payment or result, is death. This means both physical death and, worse, spiritual death or separation from God. So, God, not wanting us to pay that price, sent His Son Jesus to pay it for us. His payment covers the cost of sin and makes the gift of eternal life available to every human being. This gift is "in Christ Jesus," which means it comes through Jesus but only to those who truly call Him Lord.

The High Price of His Sacrifice

For many, it is hard to understand someone willing to die as a substitution for someone else. Imagine someone crossing the street, not seeing a large truck coming at eighty miles per hour. Now imagine a bystander willing to run out and push the person out of the way, only to be run over and killed himself. The bystander gave his life so the other person could live; he sacrificed himself.

Since Jesus was sinless, He alone qualified to be the substitutionary sacrifice for all mankind. This truth can help people understand the depth of God's love and the magnitude of His sacrifice, which can then open their hearts and minds to Jesus. Understanding the high price required to pay for their sins can also help them comprehend the value of this gift.

Understanding the high price Jesus paid can help debunk that the idea that it is easy to have our sins forgiven. In no way was it easy for Jesus to come to earth and suffer, but the plan of salvation is simple: He paid the price. It is up to us to receive this grace through faith.

Not by Works so That No Man Can Boast

Though our works can never be sufficient, the works of Jesus are all sufficient. We can never boast about our goodness; we can never presume we have earned our way to heaven. God's Word is very clear that "no one can boast" (Eph. 2:9). That means the best person on the planet still needs Jesus as Savior.

No matter how good you are, it is not enough. Yes, we should endeavor to do good and be good, but that's not the way to heaven.

Action Steps

Read: Ephesians 2:1-9

Reflection: Reflect and/or journal on how God's grace has changed your life. How does it encourage you that you don't have to earn God's love or forgiveness of your sins? How can explaining grace to people affect how they see God?

Action/Conversation:

1. Have a conversation with someone in which you tell them God wants to forgive their sin by faith through God's grace. Explain this can only be done when they put their faith in the work of the cross as payment for their sin.

LAW

Jesus Is the Only Way

Jesus answered, "I am the way and the truth and the life. No one comes to the Father except through me."

–John 14:6

KEY TRUTH

Jesus is the only way to eternity in heaven.

Imagine a sick man who goes to the doctor. After a series of tests, it is determined he needs a heart transplant to live. Many steps had previously been taken: increased exercise, diet adjustments, medicines, shunts, and angioplasty. Now the only hope is a new heart. Time is short, and the decision is made to do it.

Eventually, a heart is located, and the man is made ready for surgery. Now imagine the doctor comes in and puts a Band-Aid on the man's foot and says, "There you go; you will be fine." The man asks, "What do you mean?" The cardiologist says, "Your heart is all better now." The man demands another doctor because he knows he needs a heart transplant.

The next doctor comes in and puts a cast on his arm and tells him he will be ok. The patient demands more. So, another doctor comes in and tells him his surgical team is ready to give him a kidney transplant. Finally, the man stands up and insists the only thing he needs is a heart transplant.

No matter how well intentioned or skilled the doctors were, their efforts were misdirected. If someone's heart is failing, the only thing that can help is a new heart.

We Need a New Heart

People may make many well-intentioned and sincere attempts to reach God, but Jesus declared that He is the only way to the Father. In Acts 4:12, Peter boldly declares, "Salvation is found in no one else, for there is no other name under heaven given to mankind by which we must be saved."

We need a spiritual heart transplant, and faith in Jesus is the only way to that new heart. No other religion, philosophy, or man-made effort can erase the effects of sin; only Jesus' payment for sin is sufficient.

Jesus Is *the* Way

Many people will tell you that saying Jesus is the only way is being closed minded. To many, this assertion is offensive, but this reaction is due to a lack of understanding. All religions and philosophies are helpful to people in some way; otherwise, no one would follow them. One of the reasons people join cults is because they provide structure and community, which can be very beneficial, but this doesn't mean cults have an eternal benefit.

While every religion may offer a temporary gain, putting your faith in anything but Jesus is like trying to use a Band-Aid when major surgery is needed. It doesn't matter how skillfully that Band-Aid is applied, the real issue isn't being addressed and the long-term results will be disastrous.

What Makes Christianity Special?

People often say all religions "basically believe the same things," which is partially true. We cannot dismiss the fact that most religions encourage people to be morally good and to refrain from doing that which is morally bad. That being said, the reality is that all these efforts, no matter how noble and sincere, are insufficient. They are Band-Aids when we need a heart transplant.

In a nutshell, the difference between Christianity and all other religions is that every religion or philosophy is an attempt to earn heaven or achieve lasting peace in our own strength. Christianity boldly declares that all our efforts are insufficient; the only thing that pays for sin and connects us with God is the shed blood of Jesus. The benefits of Christ's sacrifice are received by grace through faith, not by our works (Eph. 2:8-9). Jesus is the only way.

Sharing the Truth in Love

How we communicate the truth of the gospel is very important. Our goal is not merely to be correct but to help people understand and receive the hope we are offering. Truth, by definition, will be offensive to those who hold opposite beliefs. In our human nature, we don't like being wrong, yet to accept a new truth, we have to admit we were wrong in our previous conclusion. So, be gentle in your delivery. Think of how you will be perceived and always speak with love. Too many times, people reject the truth because of the messenger, rather than the content of the message.

Gandhi famously said, "I like your Christ. I do not like your Christians. Your Christians are so unlike your Christ."[4] In a sense, Gandhi was impressed with Jesus, but not with those who claimed to be Jesus' followers. Let's look at John 1:14 and 1 Corinthians 13:4-8 to understand how we must present truth.

First, John 1:14 says, "The Word became flesh and made his dwelling among us. We have seen his glory, the glory of the one and only Son, who came from the Father, full of grace and truth." Notice that Jesus came "full of grace and truth." In biblical interpretations, there is a principle called the law of first mention. This law states that items in the Bible are listed in order of preference or hierarchy. Therefore, Jesus came with a bigger dose of grace than truth.

While the truth is the medicine needed to cure our sin disease, grace allows the truth to be received. Grace can be defined both as unmerited forgiveness and also as the power to do and be what God calls us to be. So, grace gives people space to hear and receive truth. It empowers us to change and live out that truth. Sharing truth without grace can cause people to put up a wall that keeps them from fully receiving our message.

Gandhi may have found the truth of Christ very appealing, but, unfortunately, the "Christians" he met were offensive in a way that made the truth they shared unappealing. How might India and the world be different if Gandhi had met people who shared the truth and love of Christ in a way that caused him to converted to Christianity? What if Gandhi had then boldly declared the gospel to the nation of India? How many lives were *not* impacted because Christians misrepresented the grace of Christ in some way?

It's easy to blame others, but let's be honest. How many times have we seen Christians share the truth in an offensive way? Even if it's not offensive, how many times has it been unclear or awkward? Are we speaking the truth in love (Eph. 4:15)?

Next let's consider 1 Corinthians 13:4-8a, another verse about sharing the truth in love:

> *Love is patient, love is kind. It does not envy, it does not*
> *boast, it is not proud. It does not dishonor others, it is not*

self-seeking, it is not easily angered, it keeps no record of wrongs. Love does not delight in evil but rejoices with the truth. It always protects, always trusts, always hopes, always perseveres. Love never fails.

When speaking to individuals or groups, I often tell people that the Bible says, "He who wins souls is wise" (Prov. 11:30, NKJV). This verse does not say, "He who wins arguments." Sharing the truth *in love* means being patient and kind—not boastful and not proud we are "right." If we have accepted Jesus' love and forgiveness, we received it through grace; we didn't deserve it and shouldn't lord it over another.

Sharing Jesus should never be done in an angry way or in a manner that dishonors people. The gospel is much more than a laundry list of faults to correct. We should protect people as they discover the truth and trust God to do the work. We must simply persevere, knowing that love will not fail.

Sharing without Fear

If we are committed to sharing the truth of Jesus, we should not fear people rejecting the message. We can only present this truth in grace and love. We cannot convince people of it—that is God's work. But we can be confident that, if we do our part, God will do His.

Action Steps

Read: John 14:6-14

Reflection: Reflect and/or journal about Jesus being the only way to the Father and to eternity in heaven. Also on our calling to do what Jesus did including connecting people with the Father.

Action/Conversation:

1. Have a conversation with someone, explaining why Jesus is different from founders of other religions and philosophies.

LAW

Hell Was Not Created for People

*Then He will also say to those on the left hand, "Depart from Me, you cursed,
into the everlasting fire prepared for the devil and his angels."*

—Matthew 25:41

KEY TRUTH

God wants all people in heaven with Him.

Hell is real, and it is forever; this is incredibly bad news. The good news is, however, that it was not created for people. God created hell to contain Lucifer and the rebellious angels; it was not created for people. Even so, some will still end up there. This should be frightening to people when they think about their eternity. It should also unsettle us as we consider the people we care about who may not follow Jesus.

Much of the church has been lulled into a sense of safety, for themselves and those around them. I don't believe in fear mongering and you can't scare someone into true repentance and willingness to follow Jesus, but I believe we've gone too far in the opposite direction and have reached a place of apathy. Many people have a false sense of peace when surrounded by people who are clearly not interested in following Jesus. This has bad consequences, both now and for eternity.

Punishment or Eternal Life?

Jesus told stories or "parables" to explain heavenly principles in earthly language. In the parable of the sheep and goats in Matthew 25, Jesus explains that all nations and people will be judged and divided into two categories: "And these will go away into everlasting punishment, but the righteous into eternal life" (v. 46).

Everlasting punishment or eternal life: these are the only two options. In today's world, people may reject this reality as too simplistic, but what people think can never override what God is clearly telling us. It's black and white, with no middle ground.

The Gravity of Eternity

Jesus clearly shows that, in eternity, things are absolutely cut and dry. Each of us will either spend eternity with God in heaven or separated from God in hell. Remember, Jesus used specific words like "everlasting" and "eternal." Perhaps believers wouldn't be so reluctant to evangelize if they fully understood eternal separation from God.

The reality is, if someone has not repented of sin and received forgiveness, they are still in sin, still separated from God. If they die in this separation, it is eternal. Many people give everything they have to help people overcome physical illness. Few people show this same effort to help people overcome their sin sickness.

Hell is the place of eternal separation from God, and we cannot forget its significance for each person we know. The reality of hell should drive us to reach out to those in our influence, sharing our faith so they won't end up there. It is our personal responsibility, as Christians, to do everything in our power to help people connect with Jesus and spend eternity with Him.

What about Purgatory?

Just recently, I was asked about purgatory. Purgatory is a teaching—predominately in the Roman Catholic Church—of an intermediary place between heaven and hell where people pay for their sins until they have paid the debt and can then go to heaven. This teaching also includes instruction for the living to pray for those in purgatory to "speed up" the process of that soul going to heaven.

Now, I was raised Roman Catholic and went to eight years of Catholic school. I received a great education and, in many ways, succeeded educationally because of the foundation I received. I also went to mass every Friday morning in school and again on Sundays with my family. I have a deep appreciation for the nuns who were some of the best teachers I ever had and for the priests who deeply cared about us.

Many Roman Catholics have a deep respect and love for the Roman Catholic Church. I, too, have an appreciation for my experience and the wonderful people who touched my life at a young age. With that being said, I must still address the false teaching of purgatory because God's truth is more important than man's traditions.

Purgatory is not real. This can be a shocking statement, especially to those who have been taught their whole lives that it is real. Even if it is shocking or discomforting to our hearers, we must help people navigate false teaching if they are to understand the truth.

Jesus never taught about purgatory. Neither is there clear and easily understood scripture about purgatory anywhere else in the Bible. The concept of purgatory declares that the work of the cross and the shedding of Jesus' blood is not sufficient to pay for people's sins. It states extra "work" can be done to earn a way to heaven.

It also gives people a fall sense of security as they reason they get a second chance in purgatory. Many think, "I am a good person. Even if I don't make it to heaven right away, I will go to purgatory to get cleaned up. Then I'll make it to heaven." With this theological misunderstanding, people may not feel the urgent need to repent and follow Jesus now.

Counting on others' prayers to get you out of purgatory and into heaven is like throwing a party and then hiring a cleaning lady to handle the mess. That may be a good plan to get your earthly house in order, but it's not a good plan for eternity. Purgatory also goes against the doctrine of being saved by grace through faith (Eph. 2:8-9). Essentially, purgatory declares a person can personally pay for his sins *or* that someone else's prayer can pay for his sin, but scripture declares it is not by works, so that no one can boast (Eph. 2:9).

Christ Paid the Price

Many people believe that if God is good, He wouldn't "send" people to hell, but the Bible doesn't support this fallacy. On the contrary, 2 Peter 2:4, 9 says, "For if God did not spare angels when they sinned, but sent them to hell, putting them in chains of darkness to be held for judgment . . . if this is so, then the Lord knows how to rescue the godly from trials and to hold the unrighteous for punishment on the day of judgment."

So, will God actually make people pay for their sins in hell? Yes and no. You may have jumped out of your seat reading my answer, but wait. Don't burn the book and please don't write me nasty letters. Let me explain.

First, because God is righteous, someone has to pay the price of our sins. God the Father sent Jesus to pay for our sins, so no, He will not make those who have received forgiveness by grace through faith "pay" for their sins. For those who reject Jesus and the work of the cross, however, they have rejected Jesus' payment of their sins, so they must pay themselves.

A story can illustrate my point. Suppose a man who committed a crime has to either make bail or spend time in jail. If another man comes to pay the bail, the prisoner has two choices. He can accept the person's payment and be free, or he can spend the time in jail and pay the penalty himself. If the man rejects the bail payment, it is his responsibility to pay the price himself. The same is true with our sin; we can either receive the payment Christ made or spend eternity in hell, paying it ourselves. That is the reality.

It's Our Choice

So let's review the message we can deliver to unbelievers. Hell was not created for people. It was created for Satan and the angels that rebelled against God. God loves us so much that He sent His Son to die on the cross so that we would not have to pay for the sin ourselves. However, He leaves the choice to each of us. God does not "send" people away, as a cruel task master who makes mean decisions. Rather, He is a loving God who does everything He can to pave the way to forgiveness.

Even so, He does leave the decision up to us. He wants a relationship with us, and we must decide if we want that relationship, too. A person cannot choose to love and follow Christ unless he has an equal opportunity to reject Him. If people go to hell, God did not "send" them there as much as God honored their decision to reject Him.

Law 5 teaches that God did not create hell for people. This truth can motivate us to share the gospel and give us confidence that God is working with us so each person we talk to can spend eternity in heaven.

Action Steps

Read: Matthew 25:31-46

Reflection: Reflect and/or journal about the two realities of either eternity with God in heaven or eternity separated from God in hell and how it is God's Will for all people to be with Him in heaven.

Action/Conversation:

1. Have a conversation with someone about heaven and hell. Let them know God wants them in heaven and Jesus came to make a way.

LAW

More Workers Means More Souls

Then he said to his disciples, "The harvest is plentiful but the workers are few. Ask the Lord of the harvest, therefore, to send out workers into his harvest field."

–Matthew 9:37-38

KEY TRUTH

God has many people He wants to bring into His Kingdom and all of His followers should be working to connect people with Him.

"Heavy hands make light work" is an old saying. For many, it's just plan common sense. Whenever I have a big task to accomplish, I assemble a large group of people to help get the work done. The more hands, the better. To try to do it all by myself would be an act of foolishness. Fulfilling Jesus' command in Matthew 28:16-20—going into "all the world" to share the gospel—is the largest task ever attempted, so we will need the biggest team possible.

The Great Commission

Early Christianity expanded rapidly because all Christians saw themselves as workers in God's field. When Jesus said, "Therefore go and make disciples of all nations," He was telling His followers to carry His message to all people groups (Matt. 28:19). Over time, as Christianity was formalized, there was a shift in thinking. Believers stopped seeing themselves as ministers of the gospel and began relying on the pastor or priest to be the expert.

Church members became passive listeners, not answering the calling or responsibility to share the gospel and win souls. Accordingly, Christianity diminished from the most powerful move of God ever seen into a religion more concerned about "making nice people." Forgotten for many was the believer's call to bring the life-transforming power of Christ to every single person on the planet. Simple math tells us that a few pastors can't reach all people. At the end of the day, the Great Commission is a *huge* job!

Together, We Can Change the World

A few years ago, I took a group of kids to a town in Pennsylvania to do a work camp. The purpose of this week was to gather several hundred youth and youth leaders to help fix or renovate houses of people who were either impoverished, handicapped or elderly. We had a team of about twenty people or so, and we painted the outside of an entire house in about a week. I had never painted the outside of a house and neither had most of the people on the team, but we did it and had a whole lot of fun, too. Yes, we worked hard, but it didn't seem like hard work because we had so many people.

The same concept applies to accomplishing the task Jesus left for us. If we do it together, we can get the job done—and the process will become more enjoyable, too. Our task is to "make disciples . . . and teaching them to obey everything I have commanded you" (Matt. 28:19, 20). This means bringing the good news of God's love, grace, and forgiveness of sin to every people group and every person in the world. Yes, it's a big job, but we have a big team. I have often said, "It will take all of us to reach everyone!"

What would happen if millions of people got serious about helping others connect with Jesus? I don't think it would be too hard to change our communities or even the world. God does not limit the number of souls going to heaven, but people can—if they do not do the work of evangelism. Evangelism can simply be defined as sharing the good news of God's love, plan, and purpose for our lives.

Souls Are Hungry for God

One of my favorite hobbies is fishing. Specifically, I like to fish in small ponds and lakes. I have fished so many places that I can pretty much look at a lake and know where to cast my line. Several times I have fished small, run-off ponds. People often laugh at me because "no one ever fishes" that pond. They laugh at me: "No fish are in there!" It's funny when they see me catching beautiful fish or hear my stories. I just smile and say, "The fish were there the whole time." Not only were the fish there, they were hungry and ready to be caught.

In the same way, we are surrounded by people who are hungry and trying to fill the emptiness inside. Living in New Jersey, I have been told that this is not the Bible Belt and people aren't interested in God, but I have watched our church grow from 1,100 to 8,700 in the last twenty years, with people constantly beginning a relationship with Jesus. All this growth happened while people kept telling me that God was not moving in certain places.

For over fifteen years, I preached to teenagers on Sunday mornings and Friday nights. From the suburbs to some of the roughest neighbor-hoods in New Jersey and New York, I have always found people hungry for God, just waiting for someone to reach out, love them, and tell them about Jesus. In India, while preaching in a Muslim city, I have seen hun-dreds of Hindus come forth, wanting Jesus and asking to be prayed for. People want Jesus and will come to Him *if* we will raise our voices and share the Words of life.

In chapter 1, we established it is God's will that every person comes to the saving knowledge of Christ. In Matthew 9, Jesus describes the "plen-tiful harvest" of people ready for Him. All that is needed are workers to bring in the harvest. Every follower of Christ is a worker in the field of evangelism. Before we go any further, I would like you to stop and answer a simple question. I want you to look in the mirror and judge yourself by honestly answering the question: "On the scale of one to ten, how hard am I working to win souls?"

How Hard Am I Working?

You may be feeling uncomfortable answering this question. I ask this difficult question because eternity is not a small matter. Part of spiritual maturity is being honest about where you are in your spiritual growth. It's funny how a simple question can make some defensive, feeling as if they are being "judged."

When I first got married, my wife encouraged me to have an annual checkup with my doctor and the eye doctor. Feeling healthy and having had 20/20 vision all my life, I questioned the need to go. When I arrived at the eye doctor, they did a test in which they showed me a picture of a round circle filled with colored dots. They asked for the number inside the circle, but I didn't see any number. They flipped the page to another circle; again, there was no number. I wondered what was going on.

As they kept flipping pages, the numbers eventually were clearer to me. The technician asked if I knew I was partially color blind. For over thirty years, I had not known I was not seeing all the colors other people saw. Later on, I also found out my cholesterol was too high.

When the eye technician asked me about being color blind, was she judging me? When the doctor told me I had to eat more vegetables and whole grains while eating fewer cheeseburgers and less bacon, was he judging me? Or were these people helping me understand my reality and showing me how I could improve my life and draw closer to health?

Let's deal with the issue of "judging" for a moment. How many times have you heard people say things like, "Don't judge me!" or "Only God can judge me!"? Are these statements appropriate? What does God's Word say about judgment? Galatians says, "But let each one examine his own work" (6:4a, NKJV). Other versions say we must each "test" our own works. This means we are responsible for examining our actions—not those of others.

So, how does this relate to the Great Commission? After a couple of tests that indicated high cholesterol, I made a decision to change some of my actions and behaviors so I could become healthier. Rather than being offended by the doctor's questions, I valued his bringing my attention to a potential health problem. In the same way, I have learned to evaluate my actions, examine my spiritual health, and look for ways to fulfill the Great Commission in mightier ways.

God's Word says judgment begins in the house of God: "For it is time for judgment to begin with God's household" (1 Pet. 4:17a). Judging ourselves is a way of self-correction. If we are not working to connect people to Jesus, we need to correct ourselves. We can't say we are being obedient if we are not doing the very work that Jesus came to do, namely seeking and saving the lost (Luke 19:10).

Go—Don't Just Know

This seems like the appropriate place to issue a friendly warning. Beware the "I know that" syndrome. This occurs when people gain an intellectual understanding of biblical principles, but don't put them into action. This has been encouraged by a form of Christianity that often measures growth by knowledge. The only problem with that is that God told us to "go" not just to "know."

Yes, knowledge is important and necessary, and you are likely gaining knowledge as you read this book. However, without action, we become intelligent theologians and philosophers without making a real difference with our faith. When I talk to people about winning souls, people often say, "I know that." They feel secure in their knowledge, as if no further action is needed, but action *is* needed if we are to tell the good news.

A Few Other Warnings

I would also like to warn you not to fall into the busyness of life and thus ignore your calling. Likewise, do not become so afraid of rejection or criticism that you fail to talk to people about God. I challenge myself to regularly have conversations with people about God in an effort to lead them to Christ. You might say I'm consumed with helping people connect with Jesus and with equipping others to do the work of evangelism. In fact, I'm typing right now, flying thirty thousand feet over Atlanta, because I want more people to know Jesus.

Though I am filled with great purpose, I must still be diligent in my efforts. If I do not intentionally do the work of evangelism each day, I might grow complacent—and this could easily happen to you as well. Evangelism doesn't happen by accident. It is all too easy for me to go through seasons of busyness, working ten to twelve hours every day in the church. If I am not careful, I will become consumed with administrative work or congregants' problems and neglect my job of connecting others to Jesus and training other soul winners. What is it in your life that might crowd out the work of evangelism?

It's Just Math

I remember shoveling snow as a kid. There was an exponential difference between shoveling the driveway by myself or working with my sister and father. Even today, washing dishes or cleaning the kitchen takes a fraction of the time it would take me alone if my four precious children help. If they work together for fifteen minutes, that equals an hour's worth of one person cleaning up. The work is easier when everyone pitches in. It's much like multiplying a base number by its exponent. Yes, effective evangelism follows mathematical principles.

Right now, approximately one billion people identify as "born again, evangelical" Christians, believing salvation is by grace through faith in Jesus Christ and agreeing they should be telling others about Jesus. An additional one and a half billion "Christians" identify as Christians but are nominal in their faith and do not share it with others.

If these one billion followers of Christ spent the next twelve months each winning one person to Christ, Christianity would double to two billion people in one year. When I ask people if they can believe, pray, and work to see one person connect to Jesus, it's almost always yes.

How about you? Are you willing to believe, pray, and work to see one person come to Christ within the next twelve months? You could make a powerful difference in that person's life, perhaps encouraging her to win her whole family or others in her community to Jesus. Together, we can instigate significant change.

One Is Not Enough, You Say?

Many people think winning one person to Christ is not a sufficient goal. If you feel that way, go for more. My goal is for you to begin a lifestyle of winning souls—and that starts with one. After that, keep going. The reason I challenge and encourage people to reach one soul is that 95 percent of Christians have never helped even one person connect with Jesus. That means 95 percent of Christians are not doing God's will in this area.

Chances are, if you are reading this book, you have never personally led someone to Jesus. I am writing to help you. See me as your coach, offering tips and motivation to improve, but we are not trying to win a game. We are doing something incredibly more important. We are winning souls, which is an eternal victory.

If you have won people to Jesus, I ask you to do two things. First, keep sharing your faith and helping others connect with Christ. Second, help others become soul winners. Evangelism is something *every* Christian is called to do, but many don't because they have never been encouraged or taught how.

Equipping Others

Remember that Jesus commissioned us to make disciples, and true disciples are soul winners. Famed author and pastor Charles Spurgeon said it bluntly, "Have you no wish for others to be saved? Then you're not saved yourself, be sure of that!"[5]

Sharing with others can begin with a simple statement, such as, "Wow, God has done so much in my life." Each time someone shares an aspect of faith from his own life or from scriptures, it can help others learn more about Jesus, grow in curiosity, and take a step closer to becoming a follower of Christ.

Too much emphasis in the local church is often placed on meeting the needs of existing members or helping them improve their lives. Yes, we should be doing these things, but the main role of Church leaders is to train the people within the congregation to do the work of ministry (Eph. 4:11-12).

Biblical Christianity is Focused on Others

Just as Jesus came to do the Father's will (John 5:30; 8:29), we are to continue the work of Jesus as His followers: "Again Jesus said, 'Peace be with you! As the Father has sent me, I am sending you'" (Jn. 20:21). He is sending us to seek out and tell the lost about Jesus (Lk. 19:10).

Too much of American Christianity is merely a Jesus-flavored self-improvement plan—not a plan to advance God's will and purposes on earth. The word "kingdom" is a combination of the words "king" and "dominion." In other words, God's Kingdom is the dominion that He has power to rule over. When people give their lives to Jesus, they are submitting to the rulership of Jesus in their lives.

Advancing God's Kingdom is advancing His influence in people's lives. Then these people are to increase His influence in their families, schools, workplaces, and communities. We influence others, who will influence others, who cumulatively impact towns, cities, and countries.

Many churches do many worthwhile things, but, honestly, not too many churches excel at winning souls. This is because soul winning is often relegated to the "professional" Christians—pastors and staff. However, we must remember, the congregation vastly outnumbers the "professional" Christians in every church.

The Power of a Local Church Congregation

What I am about to say will seem strange to many, but here we go: the congregation has a greater ability to win souls than the pastor. What? Yes, and I mean it. Take a congregation of one hundred people with one pastor. The one pastor has one body and one voice. The congregation has one hundred bodies and one hundred voices. These one hundred people can go and talk to one hundred individuals. In contrast, the pastor will likely be compelled to spend most of his time serving the congregation and will often be tired and overworked just from serving the hundred.

In addition, most pastors don't have many unsaved friends in their social circles. Most senior pastors have been in ministry for years and likely have other pastors, ministers, and Christians as close companions. The congregants, on the other hand, are surrounded by unchurched people at their jobs, in their communities, and among their families. The person sitting in the last row of the church probably has greater access to the lost than does the senior pastor. Put these factors together and you will agree the congregation has more opportunity to win souls than does the pastor.

Some may be offended by this truth, but I am not interested in an argument. Rather, I'm busy winning souls and equipping soul winners. By the way, my full-time job is to ensure our congregants are active in having spiritual conversations, serving people, and helping people connect with Jesus. We have built a large church of 8,700 members in New Jersey because we spend our time equipping the congregation to do the work of ministry—specifically the ministry of winning souls to Jesus Christ.

When I joined the church, we had a little over a thousand members. We have added over seven thousand people in the last twenty years, and this has been accomplished because our congregation embraces the call of the Great Commission.

Action Steps

Read: Matthew 9:35-38

Reflection: Reflect and/or journal about how many people there are that are hurting and in need of Christ. How many times have you been frustrated because you want to help more people. How would our world be changed if every follower of Christ helped someone connect with Jesus?

Actions/Conversations:

1. Commit to sharing something God has done in your life with one person each day.

2. Encourage another person to share their faith story with others.

3. Come to church each week and invite others on a regular basis.

SECTION 2

TRUTH AND MAN'S REALITY

LAW

All People Are Sinners

For all have sinned and fall short of the glory of God.

–Romans 3:23

KEY TRUTH

Every person has sinned and needs a savior.

More than once, my children have come to me, mad that Adam sinned and caused perfection to be broken. I chuckle at their indignation, but I am touched that their innocent hearts sense the world is not as it could be. They look around and see problems and know these problems are caused by sin. Eventually, the conversation moves on to something they recently did that was a sin, and their indignation changes to sorrow. It is easy to point out another person's sin, but it can be painful to see your own.

Righteousness and Sin

God's Word declares: "There is no one righteous, not even one; there is no one who understands; there is no one who seeks God" (Rom. 3:10-11). This verse teaches that no one is righteous; no one does what is right all the time. Sadly, most people lack a complete understanding of what sin is and how it damages our relationship with God and the quality of our own lives. We sin when we seek fulfillment in things other than God and His will.

In today's culture, many don't take sin literally or admit the damage it causes. Because people accept sin as "normal," many live beneath the standards and benefits God wants for each of us. In a sense, we rationalize living substandard lives.

A couple of days ago, as I was sharing my faith and God's Word, someone very close to me looked me straight in the face and said, "But I'm a good sinner." I had to hold back a laugh. Like this precious person, many of us feel this way.

As the conversation continued, I debunked the idea of "good sin" or a "good sinner." This is hard for people to grasp, especially if they are basically moral. If there was such thing as a "good sinner," this person would have been the role model.

All Have Sinned

Many things are open to interpretation, experience, or opinion. Sin is not one of them. It's like being pregnant—either you are or you aren't. You can't be kind of pregnant. A "good sinner" is still a sinner. A "little white lie" is still a lie. When speaking to someone we see as good—compared to the rest of society—we must still help them understand that everyone is a sinner—regardless of how many good deeds they have done. Ecclesiastes explains, "Indeed, there is no one on earth who is righteous, no one who does what is right and never sins" (7:20).

So, no gray area exists when it comes to whether or not a person is a sinner. If we look at scripture and apply it to people's lives, we see that all have sinned. The degree of sin or number of sins doesn't matter; we all need a Savior. To approach this topic, you might say, "You are a very good person in many ways, but have you ever sinned at all?" Usually you will get a quick "yes" or "of course" response, which can lead you to share more about Jesus' payment for our sin.

Our goal is to help people connect with Jesus, and this begins with people realizing they are disconnected from God because of sin. If people do not understand this, they may assume they are fine and don't need to be forgiven or change, which only prolongs their separation from Christ.

Obstacles to Understanding the Reality of Sin

For various reasons, many people do not feel like or identify as a "sinner." For example, some compare themselves to others and seek out someone worse to make the comparison. They may think, "Sure, I lie or watch things on TV I probably shouldn't, but I've never killed anyone." The basic premise is, "I am ok because I am better than *him*."

Another obstacle to realizing our sin state is the rejection of "absolute truth." Biblical truth has been replaced with situational truth, determined by society. Another term for this is "moral relativism," which dominates America's higher education system and culture. If someone lives according to the whims of situational truth, he may be unable to understand—or, more likely, just flat out reject—the concept of sin because, by definition, sin must be clearly defined and established by non-negotiable truth, whose concept many feel has become outdated and irrelevant.

People often say, "You can't judge me," which is really saying, "You can't tell me I am a sinner." My simple answer in situations like this is to tell people I am not here to judge, but I want them to know God for themselves and be connected with Jesus—which requires accepting His Word as the source of absolute truth.

Sin Defined

Sin can be described in many ways. A simple, practical definition of sin is something that is against God's will or is hurtful toward others. Most will agree lying, stealing, and killing are not acceptable. Sin can also be described as that which keeps us from our life's purpose.

Some sins are not so evident for those who don't know God's Word. For instance, God created us to be sexual beings who practice sex in a life-giving way within a committed marriage relationship. Sex outside of marriage is not God's will and often encouraged by things like pornography. Because pornography is addictive and may encourage the viewer to be unfaithful, many do see it as wrong. If someone trades a happy, healthy sex life in marriage for images on a screen, it is a bad tradeoff. As my friend tells people, God created us to have sex, not watch it. That observation usually gets a laugh and sometimes helps people see pornography as sin.

A technical definition of sin is "missing the mark." The word "sin" originated from a word that describes an archer missing a target. The archer "sinned." So sinning means not hitting the target, the purpose God has for us to live out or experience. People must understand sin puts us on the wrong path. It is the path of living less fully than we could and of living disconnected from God, both in the present and possibly for all eternity.

Having the "Sin" Conversation

One of the devil's greatest tools to deceive is convincing people that sin doesn't exist or that they won't be held responsible. Many Christians are scared of being labeled judgmental, so they don't address sin in others' lives. I have heard many times that people shouldn't preach "fire and brimstone" to others. I have been a Christian for over twenty years and have heard thousands of sermons, yet I have never heard a "fire and brimstone" message. I have, however, heard the truth about sin.

Because many Christians are scared of being judgmental, we are now surrounded by those whose lives are being destroyed by sin. When we understand evangelism is a process, we will realize we don't have to beat people up or get them to believe every biblical truth during one conversation. If someone's beliefs have been trained for a decade or more (perhaps by education or culture), they will likewise need time to grow to think differently. Evangelism begins with a conversation and continues with an ongoing relationship.

The damage sin causes is apparent once we learn to view sin for what it is, namely actions that go against God's will and purposes. As we share truth in love, we can trust the Holy Spirit to guide others toward this truth (Jn. 16:13). Once people begin to accept sin for what it is, we can explain our next law: sin separates us from God.

Action Steps

Read: Romans 3:21-26

Reflection: Reflect and/or journal about the reality that we have all sinned and all need a Savior and also that only Christ can make us righteous through the shedding of His blood.

Action/Conversation:
1. Have a conversation with someone about God's commandments and that all people are sinners. Share this truth from two perspectives:
    - Since all have sinned, we all need Jesus as Savior.
    - Since all have sinned, we are all equal. No one is superior to another.

LAW

Sin Separates Us from God

But your iniquities have separated you from your God;
your sins have hidden his face from you, so that he will not hear.

—Isaiah 59:2

For the wages of sin is death

—Romans 6:23a

KEY TRUTH

Sin separates us from God.

Sin is no small issue. It separates us from God in the present and can potentially separate us from Him forever. Satan downplays sin and its effects so that we do not understand or properly address it. This is like a dying from an undiagnosed disease—despite the cure and medical care having been available on request.

Like an illness, sin causes people to suffer. Sin causes God to hide His face from us because sin is a blatant disrespect toward His holiness. Many people don't know or understand this, and they eventually become mad at

God or think that God doesn't care.

Sin Ruptures Relationship

At times in my life, friends and loved ones have treated me badly, sometimes intentionally and sometimes not. Either way, I have learned that if I do not effectively address the individual, a rift will form in the relationship. A time of discussion, confrontation, and possible reconciliation must take place for the relationship to go forward. This is always necessary, even if the person had no idea how hurtful or disrespectful his actions appeared to me.

Sin, like these slights I have felt, ruptures our relationship with God. We must have a time of confession and reconciliation if we want a to maintain fellowship with Him.

Many times, sin works in a stealthy manner, but that doesn't change its effects. You hear people say things like, "God doesn't care" or "There is no God," meaning they are unable to feel God's presence. They may feel abandoned and sense the absence of His joy and peace. They may have called out to God, yet feel He has not heard or answered. They are living out Isaiah 59:2: "But your iniquities have separated you from your God; your sins have hidden his face from you, so that he will not hear."

They are separated from God by their sin and rebellion. God is not answering their cry because they are not sincere. The goal of their cries is relief from the pain of their own sin. They regret the distance they feel from Him. Yet this discomfort is merely the wages they have earned. Even though it's been almost twenty years since I started following Jesus, I can still remember the pain of being separated from God by my sin; I can remember the hopelessness I felt.

Satan and Society Glamorize Sin

Western culture has elevated sin to a degree that the ancient Romans and Greeks would be jealous of, and it continues to grow. The drug and alcohol use and sexual promiscuity that would have been labeled "fringe" and "perverted" a few decades ago are now accepted as part of mainstream America.

Movies and television programming now contains overt sexual content, vulgar language, and excessive violence—and not only in entertainment intended for adults. Exposure to these elements begins in cartoons meant for toddlers. If you don't believe me, watch cartoons with a five-year-old, and you will be amazed at what is included.

Leprosy of the Soul

Such widespread acceptance of sin leaves millions of Americans and billions worldwide separated from God and floundering in life. It is like spiritual leprosy. Leprosy is one of the most feared diseases in the world, resulting in the loss of toes, fingers, and other body parts as the disease destroys the ability of nerve endings to feel pain and thus protect these body parts.

Over time, as the victim loses the ability to feel their toes and fingers, they begin to injure these body parts, not realizing they have exposed them to danger and damaged the tissue. In some cases, rodents have chewed on a victim's flesh, but they could not feel it. Because the leper was oblivious to pain, a rodent could eat a part of a finger or toe that would never be restored.

Such is the effect of sin on the soul. It causes people not to feel and opens the door for Satan to steal, kill, and destroy pieces of their lives (John 10:10). They don't feel it right away, but, over time, they can see the damages and realize, with terror, that their life may never be the same.

When we talk to people about sin, we are not being petty or judgmental. Rather, we are letting them know they are losing pieces of their life—and will lose their whole life—if they don't recognize sin's destructive power.

Dead to Sin, Alive to Christ

Imagine the person with leprosy. Unless they understood the danger of leprosy and someone warned them the rodent was eating their finger, they would not know to do anything. They could peacefully sleep while losing a part of their body.

We cannot be afraid to talk to people about sin. People cannot get the cure if they do not know they are sick. Our goal is to echo the words of the Apostle Paul: "As for you, you were dead in your transgressions and sins . . . But because of his great love for us, God, who is rich in mercy, made us alive with Christ" (Eph. 2:4-5). We want to talk to people about life with Christ, but first we must warn them they are dead in their transgressions and sin.

Sin and Its Effects

I often speak with people who complain about everything: crime, war, violence, and what seems like a society spinning out of control. Ultimately, these worrying situations are all fueled by sin, by people missing the mark—though many don't see the correlation clearly. Remember, American society has done a lot to conceal and celebrate sin so that people are oblivious to the way it drives many parts of our society. Many are also numb to the truth on the opposite end of the spectrum, that God has a plan and a purpose for each person, family, and community and for society as a whole (Jer. 29:11).

Because so many don't see sin's part in the calamity we see on the nightly news, I like to explain that these distressing circumstances are not part of God's will. If someone is talking about violence or terrorism, I might say, "This hatred is not God's will." The same can be said for people dying of drug overdose and the rise of the divorce rate. These social ills are easily identifiable as *not* God's plan.

People also often talk about others who are making bad choices. I take the opportunity to label those choices as "sin," things outside of God's will, a turn in the wrong direction. Onlookers may say, "But he was so talented." I say, "Yes, God gave him great talent to do good things, but he got off track." This is one way to introduce the concept of sin to people who may not understand. Then you can show how, in some cases, sin can lead to literal physical death.

Conversations like this can help people learn about and navigate the concept of sin as it applies to their lives. Remember, people have been formulating their personal philosophy and belief system for decades, so we have to be patient with people as they reformulate their thinking. Many people have not been taught about the Bible, so its concepts are foreign to them. Like learning a new language, it will take time to learn biblical precepts. But in order for people to understand that they need a savior, they must know and understand sin and its effects.

Action Steps

Read: Isaiah 59:1-2

Reflection: Reflect and/or journal on the truths that God hears and can save, but our sin has caused us to be separated and caused God to not hear our prayers.

Action/Conversation:

1. Have a conversation in which you point out how sin hurts people and grows as people are separated from God.

LAW

You Can't Earn Your Way to Heaven

For Christ also suffered once for sins, the righteous for the unrighteous, to bring you to God. He was put to death in the body but made alive in the Spirit.

−1 Peter 3:18

The death He died, He died to sin once for all; but the life He lives, He lives to God.

−Romans 6:10

KEY TRUTH

People don't make it to heaven simply because they are "good people."

It's a common belief that "good" people make it to heaven and "bad" people go to hell. Most people you speak to—if you made them choose between these two categories—consider themselves "good" people and believe God would never send a good person, such as themselves, to hell. As they evaluate their lives, they focus on their kind acts and minimize their bad behavior.

Another fallacy is to view justice as a cosmic scale. If your good outweighs your bad, you deserve heaven, or at least God will let you in due to His goodness or mercy. This view is deadly because of its inaccuracy. We are either righteous due to living perfectly, which is impossible, or unrighteous from our sin, with no in between. We are either alive in the Spirit from being born again due to our faith or dead in our sin.

Forgiveness through Christ Alone

Sin is an offense that must be removed through Christ's forgiveness. Forgiveness can only be received after the debt has been paid. The only thing sufficient to pay the price of sin is the blood Christ shed on the cross; we cannot consider ourselves "righteous" or right before God based on our works. In Romans, Paul quotes King David, who also understood that God credits righteousness apart from works: "Blessed are those whose transgressions are forgiven, whose sins are covered" (4:6-7).

Law 9 is quite significant because in every religion outside of Christianity, one reaches heaven or some type of elevated spiritual state based on their own good deeds or actions. The good works earn favor and prove the individual righteous. Current deeds are seen as the way to make up for past mistakes and sins.

In contrast, true, biblical Christianity boldly states that we can never earn salvation on our own merit; we can only receive it through grace (2 Eph. 8-9). This doesn't mean we aren't supposed to do good things; rather, our deeds don't "earn" heaven for us (Eph. 2:10). As the psalmist wrote and Paul quotes, righteousness doesn't come through our own efforts but through the forgiveness of sin.

Our Sin Rejects God's "Fatherhood"

Sin is purposeful rebellion against God's authority and "fatherhood" in our lives. Sin is our signal that we don't want Him to be in charge; we don't want His help or guidance. It's a choice to go our own way. Like the prodigal son in Luke 15, we are telling God we want to do as we please.

In our sin and pride, we feel strong and independent. We think we are in charge and confidently reject God's fatherhood. In actuality, we are disqualifying ourselves as His children and losing the "right of being a child of God" (John 1:12).

From this rebellious state, we can't earn back being a child of God. This position can only be regained through faith by believing in Jesus and receiving new life, the life of His child: "Yet to all who did receive him, to those who believed in his name, he gave the right to become children of God— children born not of natural descent, nor of human decision or a husband's will, but born of God" (Jn. 1:12-13).

This is all a question of position. Each person is either in a place of righteousness with God through being born again, or he is outside of God's family. Even the nicest, hardest working person's works are insufficient when compared to God's purity. Isaiah vividly describes our sinful state:

> *All of us have become like one who is unclean,*
> *and all our righteous acts are like filthy rags;*
> *we all shrivel up like a leaf,*
> *and like the wind our sins sweep us away* (Is. 64:6).

So, all of us are unclean and outside of God's family until we reach out for Jesus. The best of our deeds and our works will shrivel up like dried leaves that are blown away. Only through Christ's intervention can we live a new life through faith.

False Faith Can Lead to False Security

Most people won't condemn themselves when evaluating their actions and behaviors, leading to a false sense of safety for both now and eternity. Their belief in their own intrinsic goodness leads to pride. The Apostle Paul warns of judging ourselves in a way that promotes ourselves: "We do not dare to classify or compare ourselves with some who commend themselves. When they measure themselves by themselves and compare themselves with themselves, they are not wise" (1 Cor. 10:12).

It goes back to the "I'm a good person" concept. You may appear good compared to others, but we all fall short when compared to the goodness of Christ. The only way a person's actions qualify as righteous is if they follow the law exactly, every moment of life, but once someone breaks it once, they are under its curse.

One Payment for All Sin

The "good person" theology is also dependent on ongoing good deeds. People may think, *If I do enough good things, they will add up over time and make up for any faults.* God's Word teaches something totally different. Instead of a multitude of little payments, Jesus made one big payment to cover the whole bill of sin: "Unlike the other high priests, He does not need to offer sacrifices day after day, first for his own sins and then for the sins of the people. He sacrificed once for all when he offered himself" (Heb. 7:27).

The surety of His completed work can bring amazing comfort. Instead of trying to be good enough moment by moment, you can live in freedom. God's Word teaches that people are afraid because they fear punishment (1 Jn. 4:18), but God's perfect love, demonstrated through His sacrifice, has the ability to drive out all fear. This kind of assurance could never be accomplished through any amount of work, personal sacrifice, or even pain endured as a penitence for sin.

No Amount of Effort Is Sufficient

Every day, people in India starve while other citizens offer food to idols. Some estimates say that rodents eat the equivalent of a train full of grain that would stretch across the entire United States because people seek a blessing and better reincarnation by honoring rats and refusing to kill them. In South America, people crawl on their knees for miles in an attempt to pay for their own sin. People in many cultures repeat prayers over and over again, somehow feeling it will please the gods or that with each prayer, God will give a little more grace that may add up over time to cover their sin. I don't mean to disrespect or diminish people's efforts, but we must be honest. Only Christ can wash away sins.

I knew a man who had been a great athlete but over time became overweight and sick with diabetes. His doctor told him that he needed to eat more vegetables. I remember watching him with a small bag of baby carrots and a big tub of sour cream. Each little carrot scooped up as much sour cream as possible. Yes, he was eating good carrots, but for every carrot, there were many calories from the sour cream, only making him sicker. It wasn't long before his body continued to deteriorate, and he died. He did good things, but they were insufficient to combat the bad.

After he passed, I went to a tribute dinner where hundreds of people talked about what a great man he was and how many people he helped, but none of that saved his physical life. Many people have eulogies that list the great things they did, but all added up, it is still insufficient to earn their way to heaven. Our best efforts can never remove the curse of sin over our lives.

All who rely on the works of the law are under a curse, as it is written:

"Cursed is everyone who does not continue to do everything written in the Book of the Law" (Gal. 3:10). Once a person sins, their only hope is Jesus, who came to break the curse.

Action Steps

Read: 1 Peter 3:8-22

Reflection: Reflect and/or journal about the fact that Christ personally suffered for our sins. How could you being willing to go through hard times or even suffer for Christ help others the way that Christ's suffering has helped us?

Action/Conversation:

1. Have a conversation with someone in which you explain that no one can earn their way to heaven by being "good" but we all require a Savior.

LAW

It's a Relationship, Not a "Religion"

I keep asking that the God of our Lord Jesus Christ, the glorious Father, may give you the Spirit of wisdom and revelation, so that you may know him better.

—Ephesians 1:17

KEY TRUTH

God doesn't want us to just follow rules; He wants us to know Him.

From the beginning, God created people for relationship. His creation was beautiful, amazing, and breathtaking. After creation of everything except people, God looked at His artwork, His masterpiece, "And God saw that it was good" (Genesis 1:25). But something was missing. Something was incomplete. Then He created man in His image, His likeness, and then God saw, "It was very good" (Genesis 1:31). Creation was complete and "very good" after God created people.

The Garden of Eden was perfection. For a time, Adam and Eve were able to commune with God in unbroken relationship. Then sin entered the scene, and this perfect relationship was broken for the first time. Since then, God has continually reached out to His creation, to those created in His image, longing for us to have a relationship with Him.

Why Are There So Many "Religions"?

Good question. I believe the answer is simple. No matter where people are, they want to be connected with God because men instinctively know God exists:

> *Since what may be known about God is plain to them, because God has made it plain to them. For since the creation of the world God's invisible qualities—his eternal power and divine nature—have been clearly seen, being understood from what has been made, so that people are without excuse (Rom. 1:19-20).*

Paul explained to the Romans that creation declares the existence of God. Likewise, the Old Testament book of Ecclesiastes explains that He created the human heart to yearn for God: "He has made everything beautiful in its time. He has also set eternity in the human heart, yet no one can fathom what God has done from beginning to end" (3:11). These verses make the following points:

1. God made the existence of a Creator clear through creation.

2. God's eternal power and divine nature can be understood simply by looking at nature. The incredible earth and beautiful people are no accident.

3. God clearly states that people "are without excuse," meaning they cannot explain away the reality of God.

4. People sense the truth of eternity, even if they can't fully understand it.

Because of these truths, every culture that has ever existed has created or practiced some form of religion. People instinctively know God and eternity are real. People are then driven to either discover truth or create some type of religious activity that expresses their need to connect with God.

What about Atheists?

Atheists, loosely defined, are people who do not believe God exists. They have come to this intellectual conclusion by observing man and culture. I have a couple of thoughts on this. First, many people who claim to be atheists are really "agnostics"; they agree to some type of God but doubt you can connect with Him, and, therefore, His existence doesn't matter. Some atheists change over time, with end-of-life confessions that either God is or might be. Overall, people will find evidence to support their beliefs and conclusions, so just because someone thinks God does not exist doesn't change the fact that He does.

The real issue is the empty space inside of us, the huge question mark about eternity that comes from our disconnection to our Creator. Man is driven to fill this space and to answer this question. Some feel comfortable concluding there is no God, while others do their best to understand and please God. If unable to fill the void with the real deal, man will fill it with something. This search for meaning and connection is the reason for so many religions. People fill the space and answer the questions the best way they know how.

Many Ways to God?

I often hear people say, "There can't be only one way . . . So many people can't be wrong . . . With so many religions, there must be different ways to connect with God." While these may be kind, inclusive sentiments, they can be spiritually devastating, resulting in eternal separation from God.

Let's refer back to one of my previous stories. When people push me on this, I ask a simple question: "If the doctor told you that you needed a heart transplant to live, would it help if I gave you a kidney transplant, a cast on your foot, a Band-Aid on your arm?" People are stunned and say, "No! The only thing that would help is to get a heart transplant." I smile and say, "You mean, there's only one way to rescue your life from death?"

Christianity vs. All Other Faiths and Philosophies

In a nutshell, the difference between Christianity and all other faiths and philosophies (even atheism and humanism) is that everything besides Christianity depends on a person's own efforts. Christianity is the only one that says, "It doesn't matter what you do; your eternal life is based on what Jesus did." All other belief systems depend on being "good enough," doing kind acts, making sacrifices, or becoming knowledgeable. In a sense, people must earn heaven, a better "next life" in reincarnation, nirvana, or simply becoming "superman," as Nietzsche wrote, by being smart and achieving excellence, which is often the goal of humanism and atheism.

Christianity is the only faith that asserts one can never be good enough to earn their way to heaven. The only way to an eternal heaven and truly living your God-given purpose on earth is by receiving forgiveness of sin through grace and being led by the Holy Spirit through relationship with Jesus Christ.

Sin is the Problem; Relationship with Jesus is the Cure

Nothing can wash away a person's sin except the shedding of Jesus' blood. Like the heart transplant story, other solutions can't accomplish what needs to be done. Jesus is very clear about the close relationship He desires with His children. For example, He said, "My sheep know my voice" (Jn. 10:27), referring to the special bond He enjoys with believers. In contrast, to certain religious people who tried to earn their way to heaven, he said, "Depart from me because I never knew you" (Matt. 7:23).

God's Word is very clear that "there is no other name by which man can be saved" (Act 4:12). And in terms of "many ways" to find God, Jesus said, "I am the way, the truth and the life. No one comes to the Father except through me" (John 14:6). If you need a heart transplant to live, you need a new heart. If a person has ever sinned, they need a Savior.

Old Testament and New Testament: Always about Relationship

The Law was given not only to establish guidelines for living well and maintaining order, but also to point people back to God and remind them to be reliant on Him. Jesus came to be the bridge back to God the Father. When a person is born again, he not only receives forgiveness of sin and enjoys reconnecting with God, but God actually indwells His children through the Holy Spirit: "Don't you know that you yourselves are God's temple and that God's Spirit dwells in your midst?" (1 Cor. 3:16).

This is not a distant relationship; in fact, it could not be any closer. As humans, we can be with each other, next to each other, connected to each other, but we are always two distinct, physical beings. God dwelling within us is much more intimate and intertwined than any human relationship we can ever have.

Heaven, then, is eternal relationship with God. Heaven is the restoration of what God originally planned in the Garden of Eden. It is the unbroken relationship God has always desired with us. Each of has broken that relationship through our sin, but Jesus paid the price for all of our sin on the cross.

Religion Can't Get a Person to Heaven

With all this being said, no man can earn his way to heaven through religion, no matter how sincere. Even though our works may be admirable in the human sense, compared to the purity of God, they are like "filthy rags" (Is. 64:6). Imagine if you owed one trillion dollars and were making minimum wage. You could never pay off that debt. Even if you worked overtime, you would be unable to make any significant dent in the amount owed.

Religion of any kind is like that minimum wage job; it can never pay the debt. In terms of becoming "wise," achieving nirvana, or being reincarnated, all human efforts fall short. History proves some of the most celebrated philosophers, artists, and musicians have ended their lives in despair and suicide. In terms of reincarnation—man's attempt to rationalize right living now for a better life later—God's Word is clear: we live once and live either with God or eternally separated (2 Thess. 1:9) from God after facing judgment: "Just as people are destined once to die, and after that to face judgment, so Christ was sacrificed once to take away the sins of many; and he will appear a second time, not to bear sin, but to bring salvation to those who are waiting for him" (Heb. 9:27-28).

I don't think we need to belittle sincere people who are trying to live well and be faithful to what they know, but we must be passionate about helping them see they need a "spiritual heart transplant," which only Jesus can do.

Action Steps

Read: Ephesians 1:15-23

Reflection: Reflect and/or journal about what is means to know God and His power. Since having the power of the Holy Spirit within you, meaning the same power that raised Christ from the dead, how do you think that can help you to win souls and see lives changed?

Action/Conversation:

1. Have a discussion with someone in which you talk about God's desire for a relationship with us—not just our obedience to a list of rules.

LAW

11

Coming to Christ Is a Process

Then Agrippa said to Paul, "Do you think that in such a short time you can persuade me to be a Christian?" Paul replied, "Short time or long— I pray to God that not only you but all who are listening to me today may become what I am, except for these chains."

–Acts 26:28-29

KEY TRUTH

We need to walk with people as God reveals Himself and they understand and accept God's plan of salvation.

Just this past Sunday, I spoke with a couple who love God and are trying to grow in their ability to help others connect with Jesus. The wife spoke what I have heard so many times: "It looks so easy when the pastor preaches and invites people to Jesus and they accept Jesus as Lord and Savior." Behind this statement is the thought, *I'm not sure I can do that.* I explained she doesn't have to "do that."

We All Play a Part

Though few people may be called to preach publicly in churches, all Christ followers have the call to be soul winners. We must never forget or downplay the spiritual process people have journeyed through before saying a public prayer or coming forward in a church setting. They may have been searching for ten years, yet we witness a moment that God orchestrated, which seems to indicate the pastor's expertise is the pivotal ingredient.

In reality, there may have been multiple individuals who talked with that person about Jesus, planting seeds that finally bore fruit when he came forward that day. Not to take away from the pastor's faith, prayers, and hard work, but remember, only God does the saving of souls, and He uses all Christ followers, guided by the Holy Spirit, to draw souls to Himself.

Paul Trusted God for the Result

Paul shared God's Word with love and boldness, but he trusted God—not his own efforts—for the result. His statement to Agrippa in Acts 26:29 demonstrates the heart we should have to all who are disconnected from Jesus: "Short time or long—I pray to God that not only you but all who are listening to me today may become what I am, except for these chains."

Paul's passion was to help Agrippa know and follow Christ. The thought of King Agrippa spending eternity separated from God bothered Paul. Even though King Agrippa and the system he was part of was responsible for Paul's unfounded imprisonment, Paul cared more about Agrippa's soul than his current actions.

Paul recognized and embraced the reality that not everyone will run to Christ the first time they hear—or even the second time, perhaps. Paul knew he did not have the power to make King Agrippa come to faith, but he had the power to point the way for Agrippa to move closer to opening his heart to Jesus. We can have that same mindset.

But I Thought Salvation Happened in a Moment

Yes, you can make the theological argument that salvation happens at a moment in time, and certain scriptures describe this pivotal moment, such as John 5:24: "Very truly I tell you, whoever hears my word and believes him who sent me has eternal life and will not be judged but has crossed over from death to life." Also, 2 Corinthians 6:2 speaks of a *day* of salvation: "For he says, 'In the time of my favor I heard you, and in the day of salvation I helped you.' I tell you, now is the time of God's favor, now is the day of salvation."

While these verses point to a moment of "crossing over" or a "day of salvation," this does not mean people arrive at this decision in a day. Rather, most take a long, bumpy personal journey to get to that moment of transformation. I like to explain salvation in two phases:

1. Pre-evangelism: the process leading up to a point of decision.

2. The moment of salvation: when a person asks for forgiveness and chooses to follow Jesus.

Personally, I can say, my life changed in a moment in the summer of 1997. Disconnected from Jesus, I walked into a church. I did not know I was disconnected or that I could be connected. The preacher asked if anyone wanted to know Jesus for himself, be forgiven of his sins, and begin a new life. I didn't have much Bible knowledge, did not even know what a pastor was, but I said yes to those questions. I asked Jesus to come into my heart, forgive my sins, and give me a new life, and that's what happened in that moment.

However, my journey is a longer story. I had decided four years earlier to find out how to fill the emptiness I sensed inside. During that time, I read many books on philosophy and religion, including New Age and Eastern Mysticism. I instinctively knew there was an answer to my inner longing, and I was determined to find it. If you saw me along the way, the things I was reading and doing, you probably would have thought I was a lost cause. However, I truly believe God honored my searching, showed me other ways were dead ends, and continued to draw me until I came to Christ. Yes, I believe my salvation happened in a moment, but there was a long process that led to that moment.

Everyone Has Taken a Faith Journey Somewhere

When you meet people, in some ways their entire life has been a faith journey. They have experiences, memories, and beliefs based on things they've been told. This history may include either many or few religious experiences, which form their spiritual reality or perspective. So, when we meet someone new, they may have a personal relationship with Jesus or may be a million miles away and against God, due to their experiences and what they have been taught. If they have spent a long time walking away or becoming distant from God, it may take time to move closer and want to know Jesus for themselves.

I often take five- or ten-mile bike rides. If I am taking a quick five-mile ride, I often go the end of my block, make a left, go for two-and-a-half miles, and turn around. One of the reasons I do this is because it forces me to cover a certain distance to get back home. If I go for five miles, instead of two and a half, before turning around, the process of getting back is twice as long.

Spiritually speaking, depending on how far someone has walked away

from God—either by lack of knowledge or willfully—it may take an extended amount of time to come back. Some people may be a million miles
from God but are so sick of how things are going, they connect with Jesus
quickly. Others may take longer, having all kinds of ideas, philosophies,
or convictions against God, Christianity, or religion as a whole. We must
see ourselves as the people who will walk with them on their journey to
Jesus—no matter the distance.

We don't have to "produce results" in terms of winning people to Jesus.
Our goal is to walk in relationship with people until they begin their most
important relationship. If we help them take one step or bring them all
the way to the foot of the cross, we must keep walking, praying, sharing,
loving, and serving them while God does the true work of salvation.

Relax, It's a Process

One of the reasons people don't share their faith, talk about God,
or try to help others connect with Jesus is fear. People are scared they
won't be "successful," with success being the other person finding Jesus in
that particular conversation. This unnecessary fear produces anxiety and
shame, causing many to shut down or run away from sharing their faith.

But when you look at sharing your faith as a process, you can relax.
You are not trying to force someone to make a decision or say a prayer
"right now." You are simply helping him understand how to move closer to
Jesus. If they are ready for a relationship with Jesus, awesome! Let's go. But
if not, that's ok.

Progress Is Success

The Apostle Paul knew that, in his own strength and speaking ability,
he might fall short of bringing King Agrippa to a place of repentance. But

in my mind, I can see Paul, with a smile on his face, saying, "Short time or long—I pray to God that not only you but all who are listening to me today may become what I am, except for these chains."

He understood that King Agrippa had been raised in a different faith system, and, though he understood the Jewish faith, he had not personally embraced it and, to some degree, the Roman Government was trying to keep Christianity under control. These factors created tremendous obstacles for King Agrippa to come to faith in Jesus in the middle of a public hearing, but Paul did not shy away from sharing his personal faith journey, not only with Agrippa but also with many others.

Acts 25:23 tells us the hearing was attended by many: "The next day, Agrippa and Bernice came with great pomp and entered the audience room with the high-ranking military officers and the prominent men of the city. At the command of Festus, Paul was brought in." Paul knew he was speaking to King Agrippa but also to many others, so he did not shy away from speaking about Jesus. Instead, he gladly and boldly declared how Jesus reached out to him, even when he was persecuting Jesus' own followers.

This is a tremendous picture of how we can deal with both friendly and hostile listeners. Paul let people know there was a better way, but he did it in an inviting manner and left the outcome to his Heavenly Father. He knew coming to faith is a process, and even slight progress is success.

Learning to See Evangelism as a Process

In my book *Let Your Voice Be Heard*, I introduced The Redmond Scale, a picture of different places a person may be in their faith journey. This is not meant to be science or an attempt to put every person into a specific category and path. It is designed to help you grasp the idea of "process," as you envision the trajectory along which people often move as they come to Jesus. The scale describes the stages through which you may walk with people.

These broad groupings and descriptions paint a picture. People you know may fit nicely into one of these categories, but that's not what is important. What matters is that you understand God is calling you to meet people where they are and walk with them over time.

REDMOND SCALE OF THE EVANGELISM JOURNEY[6]

The Redmond Scale describes general categories and possible feelings of people who are disconnected from Jesus. The role of the Christ follower is to walk with people on a journey to Jesus. On that journey, people must overcome or resolve different feelings, gain knowledge, correct wrong knowledge, and possibly overcome negative religious experiences. Though salvation happens in a moment, there is most often a process to get to that point.

7	Anti-God	Atheistic with a strong anti-religious or anti-God philosophy and negative emotions towards God or religion. Feel that belief in God or religion is a bad thing that represents foolishness or deception.
6	Atheistic	Belief that God is not real, but with little or no strong emotional bias against God or religion. View God as a fairytale or creation of man.
5	Disinterested	Religion or God is not part of regular life. They are fine if others want to be religious, but they have no interest in God or religion. May have a vague belief in God but no real understanding of commitment to God or religion.
4	Religious or "Spiritual"	Committed to a religion, spirituality, or philosophy other than Christ. This can include religions such as Judaism, Islam, and Hinduism, and philosophies such as Buddhism, New Age, or Humanism. In a nutshell, they may be religious, "spiritual," or "believe in God," but they are purposely not committed to Christ with considerable barriers to Christ.

3	Curious	Can be from any background but have come to a place where they are investigating the claims of Christ and the Bible as a possibility in their life and as something special and different than their current understanding of God and religion. Starting to understand that sin is real and a problem in their life.
2	Want Relationship	Relationship now takes priority over religion, philosophy, and good works. They are disentangling from past emotional, situational, and intellectual thought processes and replacing them with Biblical thoughts and desires. Understand sin is a personal problem separating them from God.
1	Ready for Christ	Have investigated the claims of Christ and are ready to embrace them. They have worked through barrier questions and rejected other spiritual and philosophical options. Now understand they are a sinner in need of a Savior.
0	Salvation/ New Life	True repentance of sin takes place, faith is placed in Jesus, and the work of the cross and a commitment to follow Jesus takes place. This is the starting line of a personal relationship with Jesus and the Christian life.

The Twenty-Year Journey to Jesus

I was recently talking to a woman in my kitchen about a friend of hers who had given her life to Jesus. As I listened, she told me about the twenty-year relationship she had with this Jewish woman, whom she wanted to connect with Jesus. She had babysat her children and cleaned her house. Over the years, she was a friend, a confidant, and a help. After many years, some good and some bad, this woman's walls came down, and she wanted help walking through life. She wanted to know God. After twenty faithful years, my friend had the opportunity to lead her to Jesus.

It was a twenty-year process of unwavering friendship, but it had been worth it. There were many barriers, but none too big for God. Twenty years may seem long to us, but it is nothing in terms of eternity. You can't guarantee the results, but you can be faithful to helping people walk out the process of coming to Jesus.

Action Steps

Read: Acts 26

Reflection: Reflect and/or journal about the boldness of Paul speaking to Agrippa. What do you think about the conversation and details that Paul talked about? What do you think about the concept of looking at evangelism as a process?

Action/Conversation:

1. Encourage someone to seek God in his quest for the answers to life's questions. Let him know understanding God is a process that takes time.

LAW

12

People Must Become Children of God

Yet to all who did receive him, to those who believed in his name, he gave the right to become children of God— children born not of natural descent, nor of human decision or a husband's will, but born of God.

–JOHN 1:12-13

KEY TRUTH

Sin is a purposeful rejection of God as our Father. We must choose to accept the gift of forgiveness to be brought back into God's family.

People Must Receive Jesus

Law 12 teaches it is not enough to know "about God" or to believe He exists. People must receive Jesus as both Lord and Savior. "Lord" is an acknowledgment He is the leader and in charge of our lives—the boss. "Savior" means He saves us from our sins. Most people will say they "believe in God," but this means different things to different people. The meaning can range from a very shallow, weak belief all the way to a passionate faith they are willing to die for. This statement can even refer to a different god than we know from the Bible or to a belief that does come from the Bible but is incomplete.

For instance, I went to Catholic school for eight years, from first to eighth grade. I believed Jesus lived and died on the cross and rose again. However, I had no understanding of how or why that knowledge mattered in my life. So, I "believed in God," but it was no more than historical fact in my mind. My belief did not affect my life in any way. It was not enough to bring me to a place of genuine faith, so I was still lost in my sin.

I bump into many people with a similar story; they have head knowledge but it only produces a shallow belief in God. Most are not against God and may even want to be connected to Him, but they don't currently know Him or understand how to get to know Him. We must pray for wisdom to ask the right questions and guide them to genuine faith. What may be an incomplete, surface level of belief can be the open door we need to more fully explain who Jesus is and why He matters.

People Must Believe "In His Name"

Believing "in His name" means more than people in today's culture may think. In Jesus' day, someone's name represented all he was. It embodied his reputation and carried his full authority, such that when his name was invoked, it was as if the person himself was physically present.

The name of Jesus carries all of who He is, and He was much more than just a man. He was fully man and fully God at the same time. He came not only as the long-awaited Messiah, but also as Lord. Believing Jesus existed and was a good man who taught moral principles is only part of the truth. He is God, who has the authority to forgive sin and deserves our honor and obedience. His name should evoke reverence in our heart for who He is: God incarnate and Savior of the world.

We Have to Regain the "Right" to Be Children of God

Many people say "we are all children of God." This phrase is used by people who mean well and are trying to communicate the equal worth of all people, which I agree with. While these sentiments are well inten-tioned, the reality is that when we sin, we reject the fatherhood of God. In actuality, being a child of God is a special and specific position.

Let's consider a story of a child and their parents. Imagine a young adult in their early twenties living in their parents' house. Over time, they grow rebellious. After many conversations, they still refuse to fol-low house rules and won't contribute financially or by helping out with chores. They want to come and go as they please and often create strife. Eventually, the parents must say, "It is either time to change behaviors or find a new place to live." They get angry and storm out, with a few addi-tional disrespectful comments.

In essence, they have chosen to remove themselves from the protec-tive covering and care of their parents. They have not stopped being their parent's biological child, but they have lost the right to stay in their house. In a sense, they have rejected their parent's input and oversight, confident that they know best.

Likewise, when we sin, we forfeit being God's children. He is still our Creator, but only by submitting to Him and putting our faith in the work of the cross can we regain "the right to become children of God," as we read about in the Gospel of John.

Imagine if this twenty-something comes to realize life is harder than they thought and want to go back home. Wise parents would have a long conversation and establish a different dynamic than the one that caused the separation. In the same way, God requires us to come back to Him in a different manner than we left. We left rebellious, but we must come back to Him confessing He is Lord. We left sinful, but must come back ready to be made new.

"Not born of natural descent" indicates the type of birth that gives us "the right to become children of God" is not the result of a natural, physical act followed by a normal, physical birth. No, this new birth is a spiritual birth that happens in the spiritual realm, not due to physical conception and birth.

Nobody Is "Born a Christian"

When sharing your faith, you may hear people say, "I have always been a Christian," likely meaning they were raised in a Christian home by Christian parents. This statement can mean a couple of things. It may actually mean they came to faith as a child and are truly born again. It could also mean they grew up in a "Christian" home or atmosphere but never made a personal decision for Christ.

Either way, we can discover more about the person by asking a question: "It's great you grew up in such a positive environment. Do you remember a time when you purposely committed to following Christ?" Whether they answer yes or no, we can continue the discussion and encourage them to tell their story. We can lead them to Christ if, as they speak, they realize they have never intentionally committed their life to Him. Or we can continue to pray for them and keep explaining the concept of fully following Jesus.

Cultural Christianity

According to a 2014 Pew Research study, 70.4 percent of Americans self-identify as "Christian."[7] The word "Christian," in this sense, is a broad term. Respondents are asked to choose the closest religious affiliation they have, and this term includes all Christian groups: Evangelical Protestants,

Mainline Protestants, Catholics, and even Mormons and Jehovah Witnesses.

If we use the biblical definition—a Christian is someone who has been "born again" and is a follower of Christ—the percentage who identify with the title would be much lower. We should not assume people are Christian simply because of a broad cultural term. Many people will self-identify as Christian simply because they have come from a family that has some type of Christian background. To put it simply, when they are given a form or asked the question, they look at the options, and because they are not Jewish, Hindu, or Muslim, they may decide "Christian" must be descriptive of what they are.

The Danger of Cultural Christianity

The type of cultural Christianity reflected in the Pew study signals a dangerous problem. Many think that since they *believe* in God and are basically moral, they are ok spiritually. The reality is, they are "lost" or disconnected from Jesus—all the while resting in a false sense of security that they are fine. In addition, our society looks down upon judging other people's religious beliefs and is most often against "proselytizing," which means purposely trying to convert someone.

In India, it is actually illegal for a foreigner to "proselytize" citizens. While I am allowed to teach about Jesus there, I must turn the service over to a local pastor when it comes time to ask people if they want to follow Jesus and become a Christian. In Northern India, even this is not allowed in many areas.

Likewise, in America, rules in schools, workplaces, and various organizations forbid proselytizing. In short, people often feel, what is good for you is good for you, but don't push it on me. In fact, the general understanding is that you are *not allowed* to push religion on me, with "pushing it on me" often meaning mentioning God—never mind Christianity—and encouraging people to put their faith in Him.

The reluctance of many to have open, honest conversations about faith in Christ leads to a false sense of security. Significant conversation is taboo and, thus, "believing in God," or any type of god, and "being spiritual" is often seen as sufficient. This is like someone sick with a curable disease believing that since he is at least breathing, he is ok. So instead of getting the treatment or cure he needs, he just keeps going and physically dies. So many cultural Christians and people of other faiths or philosophies feel like they are ok because they dabble in spirituality while never truly investigating the claims of Christ. Sadly, this is a mistake many will pay for eternally.

Growing up in Church Doesn't Get a Person to Heaven

Neither having Christian parents nor growing up in church guarantees someone is born again. My first seventeen years in ministry, I focused predominately on teens. During this time, I had the opportunity to speak to many teens. Sometimes, the crowd would be a mix of kids from the neighborhood, town, or city. Other times, it would be strictly a youth group where most of the kids grew up in the church. In preparation, I would often talk to the youth pastor or senior pastor; often they would tell me I would be speaking to all Christians.

Many times, at the end of sharing, I would explain salvation and give them an opportunity to receive Jesus as Lord and Savior; very often, 25-50 percent would raise their hands and come forward. This was in groups of "all Christians" who grew up in church. Going to church and having a true faith are two different things. Many people have a basic understanding of the gospel, but, for various reasons, don't connect the dots. It is up to us to reach people, one at a time, and help them connect the dots.

Born of God

Out of the mouth of Jesus, we have instruction. We must experience a spiritual birth that can only come from God:

> *Jesus replied, "Very truly I tell you, no one can see the kingdom of God unless they are born again. "How can someone be born when they are old?" Nicodemus asked. "Surely they cannot enter a second time into their mother's womb to be born!" Jesus answered, "Very truly I tell you, no one can enter the kingdom of God unless they are born of water and the Spirit. Flesh gives birth to flesh, but the Spirit gives birth to spirit" (Jn. 3:3-6).*

Only God can give a new, spiritual birth, and the only way a person can know Christ is by understanding they must become a child of God. It is not by accident. It is not through a person's parents or church. It is by grace through faith alone.

Action Steps

Read: John 1:1-14

Reflection: Reflect and/or journal on the difference between someone who knows about Jesus versus someone who has received Jesus as both Lord and Savior.

Action/Conversation:

1. Have a conversation in which you ask someone if he has purposely put their faith in Jesus and asked Him to forgive their sin.

GOD'S LOVE AND RESPONSE TO SIN

LAW

God is Patient with People

But do not forget this one thing, dear friends: With the Lord a day is like a thousand years, and a thousand years are like a day. The Lord is not slow in keeping his promise, as some understand slowness. Instead he is patient with you, not wanting anyone to perish, but everyone to come to repentance.

—2 PETER 3:8-9

KEY TRUTH

God does not force people to come to Him, but patiently draws them and gives them the choice.

We have talked about evangelism being a process that takes time. Law 13 can help us be patient during the process. One of the keys to leading people to Jesus is our constant, steadfast love and our willingness to walk through all of life's ups and downs with them. If we are impatient and try to force people to accept and digest truth in our timeframe, we may drive people from Christ instead of to Him.

God Functions Outside of Time

God is eternal, existing before time began and outside of its limitations. Modern man, in contrast, is time driven and goal focused. If we are not careful, we can treat evangelism as a task to check off. I have seen, more than once, a disgruntled Christian lamenting that someone "doesn't want God" as they huff away from an evangelism effort. Even if it is true the person is not receptive at the moment, the Christian's attitude may be offensive. We would never want a person to stay disconnected from God because of our rushed, impatient or even rude behavior. One way to look at this situation is that the messenger got in the way of the message.

When the passage in 2 Peter 3:8 says, "With the Lord a day is like a thousand years, and a thousand years are like a day," it is a poetic way of saying God is not concerned about time in the way we are. In fact, God can do something in a day that may take a thousand years in the natural world. Things we may want to happen quickly, "in a day," He may take longer to do ("a thousand years"). The bottom line is, if we want to think and be more like God, we must function, at times, without watching the clock.

God Is Patient

I am so thankful that God is patient. If there was ever someone who did not deserve God's patience because of his passion for sin, it was me. He has used me to impact many people over time, but first He was patient to bring me to a place of repentance. Before I turned to Christ, a Christian looking at me probably would have shaken his head. The Pharisaical Christians were probably asking God to hit me with a bolt of lightning! But anything I have done for God would have been impossible without His patience with me.

Created in God's Image

Since God created us in His image and is patient with people as they come to repentance, we must also be patient. In fact, it is God who gives us the ability to be patient. When God tells us we can do all things through Christ who strengthens us, this means He can empower us to be patient (Phil. 4:13).

Patience also takes the pressure off us and our time frames. Several times in the process of helping others come to Christ, people have looked at me in astonishment and said, "You're not trying to convince me!" I simply smile and say, "No, what I am telling you about, only God can do." They usually smile at that response.

Now, keep in mind, this response is after I have talked about things like God, purpose, sin, and separation from God, with nothing candy coated. Being patient allows you to *offer* truth to people instead of trying to *force* it upon them. Patience doesn't mean holding back; it actually lets you give more information to people. But then you step back as they process and figure out what to do.

New Life

Remember we are offering our listeners a totally new life, but this new life requires a rejection of their old life. However, people are comfortable with what they know and likely feel they've figured out the best way to live. As a Christian, we may see people's lives and understand that God has so much more.

Even so, people are living the best life they know how to live, and that's what we are asking them to reject. People may enjoy the things they do and be settled in their routines and lifestyles. They may also be surrounded by family and a social circle that promotes their current lifestyle, whether their current life is religious and moral or sinful and broken. Either way, if they are not following Christ, they are perishing.

New Fruit

As we walk with God over time, He changes us; we grow. One of the areas we grow in is patience: "But the fruit of the Spirit is love, joy, peace, patience, kindness, goodness, faithfulness, gentleness, self-control; against such things there is no law" (Gal. 5:22-23, NASB).

Patience sets a tone of faith and consistency. As the world continues to grow more chaotic, we can be a solid, dependable presence for others. Patience allows us to weather the storms of life in ways others can't. Patience with people lets us stand strong when everything else is crumbling. As His children, we are a representation of who God is. As people see us standing strong, people will ask us how we do it. That can be the open door we need to help people connect with Christ.

God is patient, and we are like our Father. While we are patient, we are also growing and sharing greater amounts of love, joy, peace, goodness, faithfulness, gentleness, and self-control. Galatians 5:22-23 lists the many ways we grow in the Sprit, known as the fruit of the Spirit. These verses paint a picture of how we are to be with people. We are to be as attractive and enjoyable as delicious fruit in season.

I have seen that people who "don't like Christians" over time start to like me and tell me I am not like "them." Please don't take this comment as pride. I am just saying that, as I have attempted to be like Christ, people have had a different experience than with other "Christians" who drove them away from God instead of being a bridge. God is faithful to love people always, and He is our role model.

When I first became our Church Mobilization pastor, one of the areas I oversaw was evangelism. When I met with our leadership team, one of the first things I said was that we need to love and serve people, whether or not they ever come to our church or give their lives to Christ. In essence, we must love and serve people with no strings attached. To me, that is one of the best ways to lead people to want more of God.

All Can Turn and Change

God is infinitely more loving than we are. Most of us get excited when the bad guy gets what he deserves. However, even those we are tempted to judge as the "worst" are created in the image of God. Their life may have gone terribly wrong and they may have experienced and/or done horrible things, but God is still rooting for them. He still loves them and so should we. In Ezekiel, we see God's heart toward the wicked: "Say to them, 'As surely as I live, declares the Sovereign Lord, I take no pleasure in the death of the wicked, but rather that they turn from their ways and live. Turn! Turn from your evil ways! Why will you die, people of Israel?'" (33:11).

When people turn from their evil ways, they live better lives—both now and for all eternity. They stop hurting others and themselves. God's Word in Ezekiel assures us that even wicked people can turn and change. This sets the standard; we should still go after the hard cases and continue to love those who may say they are not interested in following Christ.

The Weapon of Prayer

When people are obstinate against God, oftentimes the best thing we can do is pray. We can continue to love, sow seeds of the gospel, and pray that God softens their hearts, draws them to Him, and helps them come to a place of repentance. Whether short time or long, God will honor our prayers. He is very clear in His Word that He isn't limited by time or affected by our sense of urgency. He is patient, and our patience opens the door for God to do only what He can do.

Action Steps

Read: 2 Peter 3:1-13

Reflection: Reflect and/or journal on what you think and feel about God being patient with you and with others. What do you think is the healthy balance of having an urgency to lead people to Christ while also being patient in the process?

Action/Conversation:
1. Have a conversation with someone to explain how God is patient with people.

LAW

14

Jesus Paid for Our Sins with His Blood

In fact, the law requires that nearly everything be cleansed with blood,
and without the shedding of blood there is no forgiveness.

–Hebrews 9:22

KEY TRUTH

The payment of sin required Jesus shedding His blood.

For most of Christian history, the doctrine of the shedding of Jesus' blood was one of the most prominent and frequent messages to both the saved and the unsaved. In recent times, the focus on the blood of Jesus has decreased. Hymns such as "Nothing but the Blood of Jesus" and "There Is Power in the Blood," along with sermons on the blood of Jesus, were focal points for centuries. As churches have become more seeker friendly, powerful biblical truths, which may seem less palatable to seekers, are in danger of being neglected. However, for anyone to understand the covenant of the law and the covenant of grace, we must understand that Jesus did not come to abolish the law but to fulfill it (Matt. 5:17), and this required the actual shedding of His blood.

Jesus Shed His Blood for the Forgiveness of Our Sins

God the Father, in His justice, required shed blood for the forgiveness of sin. During the Last Supper, Jesus pointed to this new covenant, which was to be established through His blood. In lifting His cup of wine, Jesus told His disciples, "This is my blood of the covenant, which is poured out for many for the forgiveness of sins" (Matt. 26:28).

There can be no grace without the blood of Jesus. People often say, "Grace is free, but it wasn't cheap." How true that statement is! Yes, grace is free through faith, but Jesus paid with His own blood so that we could enjoy the free gift of grace. Imagine someone who took a group of people to an all-you-can-eat buffet. When the bill came, he graciously paid for the entire group. Yes, the group enjoyed everything, and it was free for them but very costly for the host.

One of the reasons Jesus held this first communion and the church fathers instituted Holy Communion as a sacrament was so people would never forget what Jesus did or take it for granted. One of the reasons people choose not to follow Jesus or follow Him half-heartedly is because they either don't understand or they take for granted that Jesus literally bled so we could be forgiven.

Jesus' Blood Is the Ultimate "Sin" Detergent

I recently spent the afternoon pulling weeds and putting down mulch in humid, ninety-degree Florida weather. When I was done, I was sweaty and my arms and clothes were covered in dirt and stains from the work. I needed a good shower, and my clothes needed to be washed in strong detergent. As people live without Jesus, they do what seems right to them but become spiritually dirty along the way. The only detergent that works on sin is the blood of Jesus. God wants us to be pure: "Walk in the light, as he is in the light, we have fellowship with one another, and the blood of Jesus, his Son, purifies us from all sin" (1 Jn. 1:7).

Along with the concept of purity, John speaks of walking in the light, which is walking with Jesus and being led by God in right ways instead of in sin. Because His blood cleanses us of *all* sin, we are called to walk and live in purity. The word "all" is key because it can help people understand God's infinite mercy and the complete work He does in believers' lives. His goal is not to condemn us but to save us (Jn. 3:17). Jesus' sacrifice was sufficient once for all (Heb. 7:27), and we are truly free: "And from Jesus Christ, who is the faithful witness, the firstborn from the dead, and the ruler of the kings of the earth. To him who loves us and has freed us from our sins by his blood" (Rev. 1:5).

Action Steps

Read: Hebrews 9

Reflection: Reflect and/or journal about how the shedding of blood is connected with the forgiveness of sin and the difference between the repetitive sacrifices in the Old Testament versus the shedding of Jesus' blood one time for all sin.

Action/Conversation:
1. Have a conversation with someone about the insufficiency of our own efforts to make our way into heaven or find peace with God.

LAW

15

Jesus is Already Drawing All People

"And I, when I am lifted up from the earth, will draw all people to myself." He said this to show the kind of death he was going to die.

–JOHN 12:32-33

KEY TRUTH

Jesus is already tugging on the heart of every person we talk to.

Many things happened at the cross. Jesus' blood was shed to pay for sins. Jesus was both the sacrificial lamb and the glorious Savior, but He took it a step further. Jesus also began a process that would make His salvation available to people by drawing them to Himself. This was a deliberate action, and He is continually at work to draw people to receive what He made possible through His crucifixion.

Spiritual Gravity

As children, we learn about gravity, the invisible force by which a larger physical body pulls smaller physical bodies to itself. If we throw a ball up in the air, the earth's gravity pulls it back. If we drop a plate, gravity says it will hit the floor. In John 12, Jesus describes a type of spiritual gravity He would put in place at the cross. Like the unchanging law of gravity, the law of Christ drawing people to Himself is always at work.

The truth that Christ pulls all people toward Himself is a foundational truth to keep in mind as you help others connect with Jesus. I make sure to explain this principle as I teach and train on evangelism; law 15 offers reassurance to believers that we are Christ's mouthpiece, but He alone draws all men.

Jesus Is Tugging on People's Hearts

It is not up to us to convince people, yet one of the greatest fears about having faith conversations is that the person might not respond positively or, even worse, respond negatively. To overcome this apprehension, I remind believers that God is already tugging on people's hearts. We can be confident that Jesus has been and is currently drawing people to Himself. When I know this, I realize I am not alone. I am not trying to convince someone to embrace something he doesn't want; rather, I am leading him to the very thing his heart desires. Jesus has started this process, and I'm just joining the team to help accomplish what He has already started.

The Tug of War for Souls

I remember playing tug of war as part of a competition back in college. We had a pretty good group of guys but needed an anchor. We found the biggest guy around, about three hundred pounds or so, and tied the rope around his waist. We gave him one direction: "No matter what happens, never move forward!"

The plan was pretty simple. If our anchor never moved, we couldn't lose. When the other team got a little tired, we would pull them into the water pit. Strong guys up front, three-hundred-pound guy in the back—it was a winning plan.

We are in a spiritual tug of war, but we don't just have some big guy in the back, helping us win. We have Jesus Himself as our anchor, pulling at people's hearts. We are simply grabbing the rope and pulling along with Him. This image gives me great confidence as I share my faith story with others.

Yes, I had confidence in my college tug-of-war team, but how much more should I have confidence in God? And, yes, we did win the competition that day. Some of the match-ups we won quickly and easily; others were a struggle. But it didn't matter as long as we won!

When it comes to souls, some people may come to Christ easily; for others, we will have to fight in prayer, with patience and longsuffering. But in tug of war, you don't care about the effort, strain, and even the pain as long as you win. We can apply the same thinking to the tug of war for souls.

On that spring day in college, there was no way I was willing to accept defeat. We can have that same mindset when it comes to winning souls to Jesus. The victory that day was merely bragging rights, but the victory of winning souls is the difference between heaven and hell for the people we love.

Partnering with God

The burden of winning souls is on God; we can't save anyone from sin. We are a part of the team, but God does the heavy work. To go back to the tug-of-war image one more time, think of a team comprised of both males and females. At times, you can just look at two teams and see one is much bigger and stronger. You know who will win just by looking. No offense ladies, but a 120-pound female cannot do the work of a 220-pound athletic male. In the tug of war for souls, Jesus is the strongest, biggest participant!

Just like that small 120-pound female isn't as strong as the big guys, she is still part of the winning team, just as we are because we are partnering with Jesus on His team to win souls!

When we picture ourselves, we may seem small, but with Jesus at the anchor, pulling people toward Him, we can't lose. I use this visual to tell people to imagine themselves grabbing on the rope that Jesus is already pulling; we are just helping Him pull. We have our part to play, but He is the one who guarantees victory.

Boldness and Confidence

With this picture in our minds, we can approach people with the knowledge of what Jesus is always doing. We can share our faith, talk about what Jesus has done in our life, and share biblical principles with confidence. Jesus is steadily drawing to Himself all those with whom we share. After we plant seeds of truth and hope, we can walk away, knowing Jesus is still drawing those people to Himself. Over time, we can continue the conversation and explore deeper questions as people let down their guard and continue to grow in their understanding of God's love and plans.

We know God's will is for all people to come to the saving knowledge of Christ. We know He is drawing them. Our role is to labor with the confidence that Jesus is doing the heavy work. We are part of His team and get to see His will be done.

Action Steps

Read: John 12:32-33

Reflection: Reflect and/or journal on the fact that Jesus is currently drawing every person to Himself and how that can help build your confidence in your evangelism efforts.

Action/Conversation:

1. Purposely have a conversation about God with someone who you know is hostile to religion and/or Jesus while leaning on the confidence that Jesus is already drawing them to Himself.

LAW

16

Jesus Broke the Curse of Sin over Our Lives

Christ has redeemed us from the curse of the law, having become a curse for us, for it is written, "Cursed is everyone who hangs on a tree."

−GALATIANS 3:13, NKJV

KEY TRUTH

Jesus literally bought us back on the cross and broke the destructive power of sin on our lives.

God's will is very clear. He never wanted us to live under the curse of sin. His passion to free us drove Him to the cross. This curse is not a one-time experience, but a path many people continue to choose, day in and day out: "This day I call the heavens and the earth as witnesses against you that I have set before you life and death, blessings and curses. Now choose life, so that you and your children may live" (Deut. 30:19).

Choose Life

God is very clear. We must decide between two paths. One is the path of life and blessing; the other is the path of death and curse. It seems like a simple choice, but the reality is, we all choose the wrong path when we give in to sin (Rom. 3:23). The choice may seem like a no brainer, but notice how the verse in Deuteronomy so clearly admonishes us, "now choose life"—as if we need reminding. If it was easy to pick the right option, we wouldn't need that second sentence. Obviously, God knew that, even with a simple choice, people could not make the right decision on their own.

As we have discussed, all who do not follow the law perfectly are under a curse (Gal. 3:10), which can be seen as brokenness, not living out our purpose, a lack of good things, and separation from God. All we have to do is look around the world, even our own lives, to see the ravages of sin and the curse. Some even say, no matter what they do, things don't go right. That is because they are under the power of the curse of sin. So many are angry at God for all the things they have experienced; they blame Him instead of the cursed road they have chosen.

Christ Came so We Can Switch Roads

Being on the wrong road becomes a serious problem if we never find the way off it. Then it becomes a permanent road, lasting for the person's entire physical life and for eternity. Once, I was on my way to Toronto with a van of teenagers, and very late at night, we missed our exit. We had to go sixty-eight miles until the next exit to turn around and then drive sixty-eight miles to get back to the same point! It was late; I was tired; and it was a long one hundred and thirty-six miles, but there was nothing I could do. One mistake wasted valuable time and caused much pain!

This story of a missed turn is a picture of how many people feel. They are tired, wishing they were going in the other direction, but feel powerless to change paths. God doesn't want people on the road of curse either, and He has provided a way out, available at any moment. He came to earth and went to the cross to provide an exit ramp, u-turn and the right road to travel.

Now imagine I was put in jail for missing my exit and did not have the money for bail. Someone would need to "bail me out" and buy my freedom back. This is a picture of what it means to be redeemed. In Bible days, if someone went into debt, he often had to become a slave to work off the debt. But there was also the concept of a kinsman-redeemer, a close relative who had the right to buy another out of slavery by paying the debt.

Christ came to buy us back, not with money but through the shedding of His blood: "Christ redeemed us from the curse of the law by becoming a curse for us, for it is written: 'Cursed is everyone who is hung on a pole.' He redeemed us in order that the blessing given to Abraham might come to the Gentiles through Christ Jesus, so that by faith we might receive the promise of the Spirit" (Gal. 3:13-14).

When a person repents of her sin and begins following Christ, she trades the curse of sin for the blessing of Abraham and receives the gift of the Holy Spirit. Christ gives us right standing—something we could never achieve on our own: "God made Him who had no sin to be sin for us, so that in Him we might become the righteousness of God" (2 Cor. 5:21).

Better Life Now and Heaven for Eternity

Many people have been turned off by some churches that portray following Jesus as merely a life-improvement plan. I agree this, on its own, is an insufficient theology and may exclude commitment to Christ, holiness, and willingness to sacrifice and suffer for the cause of Christ. However, we must not belittle the fact that following Christ has amazing benefits, both now and for eternity.

For me, I experienced true peace for the first time when I began following Christ. I received power to stop doing many of the damaging and sinful things I was doing. I walked in God's blessings for the first time. My relationships changed, and I truly began a new life. I was also able to leave behind the repetitive, broken relationship patterns that had become my norm. My current and eternal paths were changed in my one decision to make Christ my Lord and Savior.

Christ Paid for All Sin: Past, Present, and Future

People may need time for certain things to change. It may be a process to overcome the damage of sin and live differently, but they can be confident that Christ's sacrifice pays in full immediately; we are instantly forgiven and made new. We just need to keep walking with Him to receive ongoing blessings over time.

When Christ returns, He will not have to deal with sin because He dealt with it at the cross. He will be coming to gather His children who are waiting for Him: "So Christ was sacrificed once to take away the sins of many; and he will appear a second time, not to bear sin, but to bring salvation to those who are waiting for him" (Heb. 9:28). This verse assures us we can live our lives in freedom, knowing we are forgiven and have been given new and eternal life.

Part of the blessing of becoming a Christ follower is knowing the power of sin is broken and heaven is our eternal home. Fear of death leaves us, giving way to a thirst for living life to the fullest. New Testament writers wanted to be very clear on this point. For example, John offered this reassurance to early believers: "I write these things to you who believe in the name of the Son of God so that you may know that you have eternal life" (1 Jn. 5:13).

Law 16 can help us explain to people that they can exit the path of pain and take the path of life instead. As Christ followers, it may seem to be a simple choice. Even so, as Moses spoke on behalf of God and said, "Now choose life," we are God's ambassadors today. We must warn and encourage those around us to choose the path of blessing.

Action Steps

Read: Galatians 3:7-14

Reflection: Reflect and/or journal on how God has changed your life from being on a path of curse to a path of blessing. What has changed and how can God use you to help others experience this change in their lives?

Action/Conversation:
1. Have a conversation where you talk about God's Will to help people live a life on the path of blessings.

LAW

People Must Hear Preaching

How, then, can they call on the one they have not believed in? And how can they believe in the one of whom they have not heard? And how can they hear without someone preaching to them?

–ROMANS 10:14

KEY TRUTH

In order for people to come to faith in Jesus, they must personally hear the gospel from someone.

Each of us has the ability and power to share God's plans with others. Let's consider together how we define "preaching." In its simplest form, preaching simply means to communicate the good news of the gospel. This can be done in a casual conversation, in a group discussion, or, as we most commonly think of it, as a Sunday morning sermon.

Don't Put the Gospel in a Box

One of the reasons why the gospel is not being spread is that many have a narrow definition of preaching as a formal, Sunday morning presentation given by an expert. This is problematic. If we use this limited definition, many will see themselves as "unqualified" and claim to lack the proper platform to share. They will hide behind insecurity as they haven't been "trained."

I often talk about having an "evangelism toolbox" which contains different evangelistic tools for different situations. Just like a normal toolbox will contain different tools like a hammer, screw driver, wrench etc., that are each used in different situations, we should have different evangelistic tools.

Our church and evangelistic tool box can contain things like: inviting people to Sunday church, relational evangelism, service evangelism, street evangelism and small group meetings. While Sunday morning pulpit ministry should be a strong evangelistic tool in our churches, it should be looked at as only one tool in our evangelism tool box. Each one of us has the ability and power to share God's plans with others.

Yes, preaching from a pulpit is a method that has reached many and will continue to do so, but it is not enough. This type of preaching will only reach the small group of people who make it to a church on Sunday. If we are going to reach people in our broader community, we need to take the gospel outside of the church walls. We must each personally bring the message to as many people as we can.

Actions Are Great, but They Do Not Replace Words

Many people argue that they prefer to preach the gospel by the way they live. To them, I say, "That's awesome; the gospel needs to be demonstrated. However, works by themselves are incomplete. We need to use words also." I don't mean this statement to belittle people's good actions and intentions, but good actions by themselves are insufficient.

Romans 10:14 clearly gives us a pattern of salvation: Someone must believe in Jesus and call on Him for salvation. They can't call on someone they have not heard about, and they can't hear unless someone preaches (shares the words). It doesn't happen by accident. Words—not just vague thoughts or deeds—are a crucial part of the process. Some Christians assume that everyone has heard a clear presentation of the gospel and understood what they heard. This is simply not true. Many are waiting on *us* to speak the gospel to them clearly.

Gospel Words Allow a Gospel Response

For the first twenty-seven years of my life, I lived disconnected from God. I never heard a clear message or had a direct conversation about the gospel with a believer. This kept me disconnected from Jesus, even though I believed in God and, at least at times, wanted to know more about God.

I'm sure, during this time, I had contact with born-again Christians who loved the Lord and did nice things, but it never occurred to me that they did nice things because they were Christians. Observing their kind acts never communicated to me that Jesus loved me and died for my sins. No one shared with me that I could know Him through faith—despite the many nice things they might have done for me.

My response was equal to the gospel message I heard. No gospel words equaled no gospel response. I continued to walk away from God because I literally did not understand that I could walk to Him. While Christians are doing nice things to demonstrate the love of God, many lost souls will never make the connection between kind deeds and eternal salvation. They need words of life.

Words of Life

There was a time in Jesus' ministry when people deserted Him because they did not understand His most recent teaching. During the process, Jesus turned to His twelve closest followers and asked them if they were going to leave: "Simon Peter answered him, 'Lord, to whom shall we go? You have the words of eternal life'" (Jn. 6:68). Now we are the ones who have the words of eternal life. If we don't share them, people simply won't have the same opportunity to put their faith in Jesus. Not only do people need to hear these words once, but multiple times over. They may understand or receive parts of the gospel over time, eventually accepting the whole message. Our role is to keep talking and telling the story of Jesus Christ.

Words Bring Us to Our Destination

To get to a new place, we listen to the words and obey the directions given by Google maps or a GPS device. Some trips are short, with a few directions; others are longer, with more complicated directions. As long as the technology is working correctly, we will get to the destination, but we cannot get there without the right words directing us.

In the past, the most common brand of evangelism required the memorization of scripture verses and laws or rules. To "witness" you were to know and recite a certain script. For example, to share the gospel, people have used different series of scriptures and points: the Roman Road, the Four Spiritual Laws, etc. People felt overwhelmed or unable to remember these exact verses and pre-packaged details. But then the opposite happened. People now often don't memorize or learn anything with the intent to share.

In response to this dilemma, I put together a series of four points and supporting scriptures you can study to share with others. I currently use the Bridging the Gap pattern to train evangelism teams in various settings from local churches to full blown stadium events and festivals. While these points and scriptures can help people understand and choose to follow Christ, the principles that underpin my method are more important than the method itself. However, a method can help keep things clear and simple so that someone can hear and receive what is being said. Here is a summary that you can use personally or to train a group for evangelism and outreach.

Bridging the Gap

Below are key points for sharing the gospel:

1. God wants an *eternal relationship* with you.

2. Our sinful choices have *broken* the *relationship.*

3. Jesus is the *bridge back* to this relationship

4. We must *choose* to be *loyal* to this relationship.

#1 - God wants an *eternal relationship* with you.

+   "For God so loved the world that he gave his one and only Son, that whoever believes in him shall not perish but have eternal life" (Jn. 3:16).

+   "I keep asking that the God of our Lord Jesus Christ, the glorious Father, may give you the Spirit of wisdom and revelation, so that you may know him better" (Eph. 1:17).

+   "For in him all things were created: things in heaven and on earth, visible and invisible, whether thrones or powers or rulers or authorities; all things have been created through him and for him" (Col. 1:16).

Explanation: God wants us to personally know Him, not just know *about* Him. He loves us so much that He literally sent His Son to die on the cross for us. When we put our faith in Jesus and the work He accomplished on the cross, God will forgive our sins and give us eternal life. He not only wants us to know Him in eternity but on a daily basis right now. We were created for relationship with God.

#2 - Our sinful choices have *broken* the *relationship.*

- "For all have sinned and fall short of the glory of God" (Rom. 3:23).

- "For the wages of sin is death" (Rom. 6:23a).

- "But your iniquities have separated you from your God; your sins have hidden his face from you, so that he will not hear" (Is. 59:2).

Explanation: Every single person has made wrong decisions and done wrong things. God calls these things "sin," and they separate us from God relationally and cause a spiritual death within us. When this relationship is broken, God does not hear us because we have walked away from Him.

#3 - Jesus is the *bridge back* to this relationship.

- "Very truly I tell you, whoever hears my word and believes him who sent me has eternal life and will not be judged but has crossed over from death to life" (Jn. 5:24).

- "Jesus answered, 'I am the way and the truth and the life. No one comes to the Father except through me'" (Jn. 14:6).

134

- "But the gift of God is eternal life in Christ Jesus our Lord" (Rom. 6:23b).

Explanation: Imagine a person standing at the top of one side of the Grand Canyon. He wants to walk across to the top of the other side, but with no bridge, it's impossible to walk across this gap. The gap caused by sin is even greater, but Jesus is the bridge that can allow a person to go across that gap. Not only is He the bridge, He is the only bridge. Only He died to pay for the sins of man, and only He can give the gift of eternal life.

#4 - We must *choose* to be *loyal* to this relationship.

- "Yet to all who did receive him, to those who believed in his name, he gave the right to become children of God" (Jn. 1:12).

- "Greater love has no one than this: to lay down one's life for one's friends. You are my friends if you do what I command" (Jn. 15:13-14).

Explanation: Like any personal relationship, we have to make a choice to be in the relationship. When we choose to sin, we choose separation and choose not to be God's child. When we receive Jesus by believing He is the Savior, we regain the right to be God's child. We stay in right relationship and close to Jesus when we are obedient to His teachings in the Bible.

By understanding and knowing these scriptures and principles, you can weave these spiritual truths into your conversation to help people come to Jesus. By sharing the principles above, you are "preaching" the gospel to others. They are being presented with a clear picture and pathway to overcome sin and have a personal relationship with Jesus.

Action Steps

Read: Romans 10:1-15

Reflection: Reflect and/or journal your thoughts about the power of our words as discussed in Romans 10. It speaks of the power of leading someone to Christ by what we say and how salvation can be received when people speak faith filled words.

Action/Conversation:

1.   Have a conversation with someone whose life is not going in the direction he wants. Then speak life to them by telling them God has more for their life.

SECTION 4

MAN'S RESPONSE TO GOD'S LOVE

LAW

We All Have a Ministry of Reconciliation

*Therefore, if anyone is in Christ, the new creation has come: The old has gone,
the new is here! All this is from God, who reconciled us to himself through
Christ and gave us the ministry of reconciliation.*

−2 COR. 5:17-18

KEY TRUTH

*God provides us with the message. After we receive the message, He continues
the process by sending us to others so they can hear the message.*

Out with the Old

Christ didn't die on the cross and rise again so we could attend some
religious services. He came so we could literally be recreated, born again a
different person. The old person who lived disconnected from God is gone.

When we were separated from Jesus, we walked a path that made us
less and less like Jesus over time. Our offensiveness to God grew with each
sin. But God did not want to leave us in that state. He is all about making
sure we experience new life, so He sent Jesus to step in to resolve the sin

issue that separated us from Him.

Once an issue is handled or offense has been taken away, people can be reconciled. To reconcile means to settle a quarrel or dispute or to bring into harmony or agreement.[8] Christ came to bring us into harmony with the Father by settling the offense caused by our sin. When we are born again, we are filled with the Holy Spirit, which transforms us to be more like Christ. We become compatible with God and behave like Him more consistently.

Receive, Grow, Give It Away

Years ago, I came up with the statement "receive, grow, give it away" to help others understand what God wants us to do with many of the gifts He gives us. First, we must receive them. God wants to give us more than we know. If we could learn to be better receivers, many of our lives would be changed. Once we receive things from God, we can then grow in those things. If God gives us peace or wisdom, we can grow in those gifts so that they impact many areas of our lives. God's Word even teaches us that we need to "grow up in our salvation" (1 Pet. 2:2). Then the third part of this formula is to give it away. God doesn't want us to hold on to the things He gives us; rather, He wants us to share them with others and help them experience His gifts also.

Everyone Has the Ministry of Reconciliation

People often wonder what they should be doing for God. We often think of ministry in terms of "public ministry," such as preaching or singing in the choir on Sunday morning. This definition can be limiting because it restricts ministry to a small gift set, comprised of tasks many are not called to do—at least not on a Sunday morning. Ministry can instead be understood as serving or helping people on God's behalf. Most of our service will not be public and few, if any, will know about our acts.

Look again at 2 Corinthians 5:17, our passage for law 18: "If anyone is in Christ, the new creation has come." Note the key word "anyone." Then note the process outlined: "Who reconciled us to himself through Christ and gave us the ministry of reconciliation." First, God reconciles us to Himself through Christ. Then, He gives us the ministry of reconciliation. It is the ministry of *all* Christ followers to be actively living and working to help others reconcile with God.

No Special Talents Required—Just a Caring Heart

Every believer can help others be reconciled to God; all it takes is a caring heart. I love when God uses words like "anyone" and "all" because I qualify and so do you. Consider a marriage counselor who meets with a couple to help them resolve their issues and learn to live differently. The counselor does not have the power to "fix" things, but she is needed because, on their own, the couple hasn't been able to figure out their relational struggles. The counselor can offer strategies and help them navigate the process of healing.

Our role is to meet with people who are out of relationship with God. In our own strength, like the marriage counselor, we can't "fix" this relationship. Our role is to point them to Jesus, who is the Father's ultimate "plan and strategy" to bring people to Himself. People must choose this relationship and accept the work of the cross. Our role is to offer Jesus and help them navigate the process. The good thing is, we don't have to be "talented" to do this.

In the early church, there was not a stratified structure of "experts" and "spectators," in which certain people were called to do ministry while others listened to their wisdom only for self-edification. From its beginning, Christianity was a face-to-face, relational religion in which believers personally encouraged others to have a relationship with Jesus. Out of human friendships, the path to relationship with God began.

Yes, there were leaders, such as elders and then bishops, but everyone was seen as a messenger of reconciliation in the marketplace and in their social times. Everyday relationships were a tool for connecting people to Jesus. Over time, a church structure of "leaders" and congregation was established, and one of the negative outcomes was that the leaders were considered "ministers" while the people who attended church mainly became listeners.

The early church exploded and eventually overtook the Roman Empire, not because of talented preachers, but because of people embracing the ministry of reconciliation in their lives. Talented preachers are not bad in any way, but are less effective when those who listen retreat to being spectators, instead of engaging the culture for Christ in their everyday lives.

Few Preachers, Many Ministers

The vast majority of people reading this book will never stand in front of a pulpit on Sunday morning to speak to a congregation, and that's ok. Everyone reading this book, however, has the ability to help people spend eternity in heaven because God has commissioned them in the "ministry of reconciliation." Since God has already given the assignment, my message to you is "go." As Christ said, "Go into all the world and make disciples" (Matt. 25:19).

The church lacks power because they are too often waiting for people to come to the church building instead of sending the people of God to go into the world. If a church has one hundred people in it, the pastor often gives his life to serving those people. He teaches, preaches, and visits, truly doing a multitude of great things, but he is only one person. God's plan is that after the pastor preaches to the hundred, they must then go out to the community to help reconcile people to Him.

The Holy Spirit Is with Us

The question is almost insulting in its simplicity, "Who can reach more people, one pastor or one hundred people?" If you look at personal, one-on-one conversations outside the church walls, the pastor can only speak to one person at a time while the hundred-person congregation can speak to one hundred people at a time and serve in the ministry of reconciliation. It's not any more complicated than that.

One of the amazing things Jesus told his disciples was that it was good for Him to go back to the Father: "But very truly I tell you, it is for your good that I am going away. Unless I go away, the Advocate will not come to you; but if I go, I will send him to you" (Jn. 16:7). The disciples must have been scratching their heads, thinking, "How can your going away be good?" However, when He went to be with the Father, the Father was going to send the Holy Spirit to dwell in all His followers. This meant the presence of God would go with all of His children.

Because Jesus chose to dwell in one body, He was like the pastor who could only be in one place at one time. When Jesus went back to the Father, the Holy Spirit was sent, and now Jesus' followers are like the hundred people in the congregation who can go in many different directions and speak to many people all at the same time.

If you are the pastor, I want to say thank you for all you do. I am a local church pastor also. I encourage you to keep reconciling people to God. If you are a church member, I encourage you to see yourself as a minister of reconciliation and to help people connect with God. In the big picture, it's not an "either/or" scenario; it's "both/and." God wants pastors to continue doing great things, *and* He wants all congregants to step out of the pews and minister in the community. We have much work to do and many souls to reach. We can truly impact the world when we personally embrace the Holy Spirit's power that makes us ministers of reconciliation.

Action Steps

Read: 2 Corinthians 5:11-21

Reflection: Reflect and/or journal about the idea that all Christ followers have the ministry to reconcile people to God. How would the world be different if every Christian was regularly helping people to connect with Jesus in a personal relationship?

Actions/Conversations:

1. Write out your salvation story in a long version with all the details and circumstance you can remember.

2. Tell your salvation story to three people who know Jesus to practice and receive encouragement.

3. Share parts of your story or your whole story with someone who doesn't know Jesus.

LAW

We Are God's Ambassadors

We are therefore Christ's ambassadors, as though God were making his appeal through us. We implore you on Christ's behalf: Be reconciled to God.

—2 Cor. 5:20

KEY TRUTH

God has called every Christian to actively share His love and plan with people.

Being an ambassador is a very prestigious thing. It seems that the average Christian does not understand and appreciate the honor God is calling us to. So much of Christianity has become head knowledge. People feel that if they possess the head knowledge, that is sufficient and they have done well. However, that is not what God desires. The Apostle Paul is not writing to the Corinthians so they can *know* something; he is writing to them so they can understand that God wants them to *do* something. God wants us to be His ambassadors. Let's look at what an ambassador does.

The Job of an Ambassador

An ambassador is the president's highest-ranking representative to a specific nation or international organization abroad.[9] Ambassadors maintain the citizenship of their home country while living in another country. They speak on behalf of their president and entire native country.

In terms of Christianity, our home is heaven, and we represent God. Our citizenship is heaven, not the United States or some other country. Our words and actions are to be driven by the interests of God as we speak on His behalf.

The ambassador's main focus is to know and appreciate all of the details of the culture to which he is sent; he studies how the foreign country functions so he can work with the country to achieve the objectives of his homeland. He is an expert on the foreign country he is in, but his main goal is always to advance the purposes of the country that sent him.

Our job is to be an expert on the people we know and the places we work with the main goal of advancing God's purposes. Our objective is to advance God's objectives. Each day, we are to protect and promote the interests of heaven.

Christ's Ambassadors Are Compelled by Love

Let's take a look at 2 Corinthians 5 to get a more complete understanding of being Christ's ambassador. The chapter begins by describing the difference between our earthly, physical bodies and our heavenly bodies. Verse 1 refers to our body as an "earthly tent" that will be destroyed, in contrast to an "eternal house" in heaven not built by human hands. Paul then continues to write that it will be better for us to be in heaven. In verse 10, he speaks of the judgment seat of Christ, where we will face judgment. As he continues, he speaks of the new life available through His death: "For Christ's love compels us, because we are convinced that one died for all, and therefore all died. And he died for all, that those who live should no longer live for themselves but for him who died for them and was raised again" (vs. 14-15).

As Christ's ambassadors, each of us is to be compelled by the same love that drove Christ to die for all. "All" means Christ loves each and every person so much that He laid down His life. Some have said, "If you were the only person alive on earth, Christ would have died for you." This is saying each and every person we come across is loved by God to this degree.

Verse 15 then shows a shift that should take place once a person receives this new life. We should "no longer live for ourselves" but for Jesus who died and rose again. As an ambassador, we shift from being self-centered to representing the interests of God. His interests become our interests, and our purpose is to achieve His purpose.

Ambassadors Are Ministers of Reconciliation

The shift of focus begins when we receive this new life for ourselves and become a new creation:

> *Therefore, if anyone is in Christ, the new creation has come:*
> *The old has gone, the new is here! All this is from God,*
> *who reconciled us to himself through Christ and gave us the*
> *ministry of reconciliation; that God was reconciling the world*
> *to himself in Christ, not counting people's sins against them.*
> *And he has committed to us the message of reconciliation*
> *(2 Cor. 5:17-19).*

When old things go away, we shift from being self-absorbed to focusing on others. Our interests get replaced with God's interests. Our self-absorption gets replaced by a burden for those around us; we have the ministry of reconciliation to those disconnected from Jesus.

This doesn't mean all of our life circumstances will change. We may not change our workplace, where we live, or many of our daily tasks, but we will experience a fundamental shift in how we view others. We are no longer wasting time or living for the next paycheck; rather, we live to advance God's agenda as His ambassador. In this process, our ultimate goal is to help individuals reconcile with God.

"Reconciliation" is a noun for the act through which enemies become friends.[10] As an ambassador focused on reconciling people to God, we bring people who are disconnected from God, "enemies" through the offense of their sin, back to Him. We help people understand they can be compatible with God and enjoy a relationship with Him because of what Christ did on the cross.

On Jesus' behalf, we tell others the good news that He is not counting their sins against them. He has paid the price for sin, making it as if it never happened. People don't need to be fearful of God or controlled by the regret of their sin. Christ came from heaven to remove the offense of sin and the punishment of separation from God.

We are the bridge between broken, disconnected people and Jesus. Our role is to communicate God's love and plan to others. To do so, we learn and infiltrate the culture or "country" we live in. Our interests are now to help others walk in the true purpose of why they were created. We must share the message of reconciliation so that individuals can receive forgiveness and receive new life. We are helping them change their citizenship from this broken world to God's perfect Kingdom.

Overcoming the Offense of the World

I have been amazed at how offended some people can be by people's actions, to the degree that they want to totally avoid them instead of being ambassadors to help them be reconciled to God. I often say, "Sinners sin; liars lie; stealers steal; that's what they do."

Instead of being offended by and retreating from the world, we must get involved, try to understand people, and work to successfully communicate God's plans to them. Others' sinful actions should motivate us to help them change or, more accurately, be changed.

When Christ gives people new life, their behaviors, actions, and words will change. Yes, it can be hard at times to love the unlovely, but Jesus never shied away from sinners. Rather, He engaged them and helped them receive new life. It is the old, broken life that causes people to act the way they do. This is why Jesus sends us to engage with people and help them change life paths.

Reaching Millions One by One

One of the reasons God calls each of us to be His ambassador is because millions are disconnected from Jesus. God is calling each of His children to engage people in their lives as an ambassador of Christ. Each of us can connect with people we already know in our families, schools, workplaces, and communities.

You likely know people without a church, of a different faith, with no faith, or who walked away from church for a myriad of reasons. No matter their current story, we can be Christ's ambassador and help them along the journey of reconciliation. Our job is to share truth in love, walk with people, help them process scripture, and pray that God continues to draw them. In this process, we must see ourselves as Christ's ambassador.

Action Steps

Read: 2 Corinthians 5:11-21

Reflection: Reflect and/or journal on how you feel about being an "ambassador for Christ". How do you feel about the idea that it is your responsibility to speak on Christ's behalf?

Action/Conversation:
1. See yourself as someone speaking on God's behalf as you talk to people this week.

LAW

We Must Share Both Good and Bad News

*How, then, can they call on the one they have not believed in? And how can they
believe in the one of whom they have not heard? And how can they hear without
someone preaching to them? And how can anyone preach unless they are sent?
As it is written: "How beautiful are the feet of those who bring good news!"
But not all the Israelites accepted the good news. For Isaiah says, "Lord, who
has believed our message?" Consequently, faith comes from hearing the
message, and the message is heard through the word about Christ.*

–ROMANS 10:14-17

KEY TRUTH

People must hear a clear gospel message to believe.

In writing to the Romans, Paul asks powerful questions to spur his
readers toward evangelism. The quick answer to all the questions has
asked is, "They can't." The gospel message contains both good and bad
news. The good news is simple. Christ loves us, has a plan for us and died
on the cross to pay for our sins to pave the way for forgiveness and eternity
with God in heaven. The bad news is also simple. Without receiving forgiveness for our sins through faith, there will be separation from God both

on a daily basis now, but even worse, for eternity in hell. God's Word is very clear on these two eternal places the only question is which one each person will spend eternity in. It is our responsibility to share this truth in love with the people in our lives.

Believing Is the Key to Salvation

No one can call on Jesus if they have not believed in Him. Believing in Him goes beyond knowing He exists or being religious in some way. I had a basic understanding of who Jesus was from attending Catholic School, going to mass every Friday, and attending church on Sundays with my family. These religious exercises helped me know a historical Jesus, but I did not understand why He came and why it could make a difference in my life. I had no problem with God's existence and thought He might even be available to me at times, but I was disconnected from Him because I had no strong belief or conviction.

Like countless people, I had a form of religion but it fell short of true faith in Christ. Paul observed the same behavior in first-century believers: "Holding to a form of [outward] godliness (religion), although they have denied its power [for their conduct nullifies their claim of faith]" (2 Tim. 3:5, AMP).

I had a "form" of religious belief, but it had no impact on my life because I did not understand I was a sinner in need of a Savior. I did not realize my separation from God and the emptiness inside was from my own actions. I did not know Christ died for my sins so I could receive forgiveness. No one had explained God's love and plan of salvation for my life. I did not reject believing; I did not know there was something to believe because no one preached to me. It was not until I started going to a church that taught from the Bible that I understood the good news of the gospel.

The word "evangelize" means "to share the good news," as in Romans

10:15b: "How beautiful are the feet of those who bring good news!" This verse paints a picture of the military messenger of the day. When an army went out to battle and were victorious, they would often send a messenger ahead to proclaim the victory. He usually came on foot, so they would say, "His feet are beautiful!" because he brought the good news of victory. The Apostle Paul then paints the picture of someone who brings the good news of the victory of Jesus Christ.

Those who are disconnected from Jesus may be successful (by the world's standards) or struggling to get by, but either way, without the victory of Christ, their current life will eventually fall apart and their eternity will be separation from God. The good news must be shared.

The Pulpit Is Only One Place of Sharing

I thank God for the many great preachers who share God from the pulpit each Sunday morning. In fact, I'm one of them. But the reality is, the church is overly reliant on Sunday-morning sermons. Yes, we should continue to meet on Sunday mornings to worship and hear biblical teaching, but we need a greater focus on sharing the good news throughout the week in regular settings. Let's consider how the early Church spread the news of Christ's resurrection:

> *Every day they continued to meet together in the temple*
> *courts. They broke bread in their homes and ate together with*
> *glad and sincere hearts, praising God and enjoying the favor*
> *of all the people. And the Lord added to their number daily*
> *those who were being saved (Acts 2:46-47).*

The early church spread the word in the temple courts and met in homes, spending time together encouraging one another. The result was that God added to their number "daily" those who were being saved. This is God's heart that people meet face-to-face to praise God and tell others about the good news. We are not to wait for the lost to attend the church building; we *are* the church. We must bring the good news to them.

Relational evangelism is still the greatest way to help people get connected with Jesus and to help people come to church. 86 percent of people who visit a church come due to a personal invitation from someone they know.[11] But in order for the church to impact more lives and shape culture once again, the members of our churches must share the good news outside the walls of church.

Evangelism through Relationship

Each day we hear of the unfortunate consequences that come to people who have not received and accepted the good news of Jesus Christ. After the Orlando Massacre occurred on June 12, 2016, with forty-nine people killed at the Pulse nightclub, I sat with my mom and talked about what had happened. I wondered aloud what might have been different if someone had shared the gospel with Omar Mateen, the shooter.

If he had allowed Christ to redirect his life and heal his brokenness, he could have spent his life helping people instead of ending forty-nine young lives. We can conquer darkness with light, but the message of Christ must be proclaimed to be heard: "Consequently, faith comes from hearing the message, and the message is heard through the word about Christ" (Rom. 10:17).

Yes, the massacre is an extreme example, but my point is true. For years I have seen God transform people—hard-working, fairly moral people and also alcoholics, gang members, and others who sin like it's an extreme sport. God is able to change any heart *if* we share the good news. People are looking; they are hungry; some are desperate; and we have the answer if we will let our voice be heard.

The outcome of sharing the Word about Christ is transformed lives on this side of eternity and eternal life in heaven with Christ. We are surrounded by people each day who are looking for answers. Most are like I was; they are not against God but just don't understand how God can truly impact their lives. They have not heard the good news, or, if they have, no one has walked with them to process it until they understand.

This is why evangelism through personal relationship is so important. Many seekers go to church and may like much of what they hear, but they probably have many questions. The gospel may seem foreign or not real to them at first. We must spend time in conversation and community, asking questions and explaining Jesus' gift of salvation. If we proactively and purposely spend time building relationships with others, over time, it will be natural to have spiritual conversations.

Technology Cannot Replace Relationship

The past fifty years has seen technological advances that have radically changed our lives. We can now communicate and share information quickly, in ways never dreamed of. In spite of these advancements, Christianity has remained roughly the same percentage of the world population over the forty-year period from 1970 to 2010. To be clear, I want to encourage all methods of sharing the gospel, whether it be traditional church, internet, television, radio, Christian concerts, etc. However, the reality is, if we want to see the Great Commission fulfilled, we need every Christian sharing the good news through face-to-face interactions with people.

Yes, I tweet and see some benefits from maintaining a social media presence, but people are longing for relationship and deeper connection than can be achieved in 140 characters. If every Christ follower spent the next twelve months helping one person hear, understand, and accept the good news of Jesus Christ, Christianity could double in one year. Maybe everyone won't embrace this idea, but you can. Will you commit the next twelve months to praying for and talking to at least one person with the belief that she will hear and receive the good news of Jesus and accept Him as Lord and Savior?

I don't know how beautiful your feet are, but I pray they become more beautiful in the days ahead!

Action Steps

Read: Romans 10:13-17

Reflection: Reflect and/or journal your thoughts on the reality is that we are surrounded by people who have not clearly heard the message of the gospel. What do you see as your responsibility in sharing the gospel with people?

Action/Conversation:

1. Have a clear conversation with someone in which you speak of the reality of both sin and God's grace.

2. Commit the next 12 months of your life to winning at least one person to Jesus.

LAW

We Are Living Epistles

*You yourselves are our letter, written on our hearts, known and read by
everyone. You show that you are a letter from Christ, the result of our
ministry, written not with ink but with the Spirit of the living God, not on
tablets of stone but on tablets of human hearts.*

—2 COR. 3:2-3

KEY TRUTH

Our lives are a message to people about God.

Throughout time, letters have been a key form of communication, not
only to share information but also to capture a person's heart in a concise
way. For centuries, letters were the only way to communicate about life's
most important matters.

Because God's wants to share His plan with others through His
children, the Apostle Paul equates believers with letters that communicate
the good news. God's Words are written on our hearts and read by others when our lives reflect God's love and grace. We are an open book that
explains the reality and love of God. We are literally God's love letter, with
His word written on our hearts by the Holy Spirit. Once again, this is ev-

ery Christian, not just a chosen few. Let's take a deeper look at this truth.

Written on Our Hearts

As people are looking for answers to life's toughest questions, God is sending us out, equipped with the answers about the meaning of life, connecting with God, and navigating life's challenges. God writes these answers on our hearts so that we can speak them: "For the mouth speaks what the heart is full of" (Lk. 6:45).

We speak from whatever fills our hearts, and everyone around us will hear. We are an open letter. This is a picture of the church bringing the gospel to the world, instead of trying to just gather people to a church service. They didn't have billboards in Jesus' day, but imagine yourself as a Jesus advertisement. We are ambassadors, spokesmen, and God's love letter to the people in our lives. Let's look at how you can grow in sharing the story of your personal encounter with the gospel.

Write out Your Story

One of the most powerful tools for leading others to Christ is sharing your personal faith story. Please see resource 1 in the back of the book, which outlines a thirty-minute interactive discussion we lead groups through each month at our church called *Sharing Your Story*. This exercise helps people start thinking about and preparing their story; we see many grow in their ability to share their personal faith journey.

So, the first step is to write out a long version of how you came to know Christ. Refer to section 3 in *Sharing Your Story* for a list of questions to help you get started. Be sure to include what life was like before Christ, the circumstances that brought you to Him, your "aha" moment, and how Christ changed your life. This is a powerful process for every believer because it is a reminder of all that God has done. It is a faith-building activity and also therapeutic.

It is amazing to see how God ministers to people in the process of writing out what He has already done. They are filled with hope that God will continue working on areas of their life. They are grateful and inspired to share the goodness of God—goodness they can prove by pointing to what He has done in their lives. So, I encourage you to write out a long, messy version of your life story and how you came to Christ. Some people write a page or two; others write up to ten pages. Length doesn't matter as much as the sincerity of your effort and the process of putting words to your feelings and experiences.

Your Story Becomes Your Tool Box

Many people have some type of tool box in their home for minor repairs. Professional contractors need to have a well-supplied tool box and may even have a tool chest on their truck. The reason they have a tool box is because different jobs require different tools. A loose screw needs the right screw driver. A nail needs a hammer. To loosen a bolt, you need a specific wrench. You get the idea.

When it comes to sharing your faith journey, the long version of your testimony is your tool box. The smaller components of your story can be used selectively to talk to individuals who may find that part relevant. For example, I am well educated, so when sharing with someone who values education, I use that tool to connect. I drank heavily for over ten years, so that is a point of connection with others. All of my background and experiences are possible bridges to different people. My story is my tool box and so is yours.

Your Story Is Powerful Because It's Yours

In reality, certain people are more likely to listen to some people over others. God's power can enable you to reach anyone, but the truth is, shared experiences and similar background can open the door to reach certain people. Every Christ follower needs to be ready to share her faith story because it is unique and will resonate with someone else like no other story can.

For seventeen years as a white man, I worked predominately with black teens. God used me to reach many, but one of my key tools in reaching inner-city black teens was other inner-city black teens. The teens who knew me understood that I loved them and were open to me, but many of their friends were not. Their friends needed to hear a faith story they could relate to, that of another inner-city youth who had met Jesus.

As I write this, I am planning to go to Nicaragua and India to train pastors who will, in turn, serve local villages I will never have the opportunity to visit. This is one of the amazing things about the Body of Christ. Each person has unique opportunities according to where God has placed him and the influence he has with certain people.

Don't worry about whether your story is particularly interesting. Some people have dramatic stories of how they came to Christ, but many don't. To put it bluntly, few people appreciate their own story as much as they should. It's like listening to yourself on an audio recording; most people don't like how they sound. In the same way, others' stories often seem more appealing or interesting than ours, and dramatic conversions are shared publically and even publicized.

Let me assure you of two things. First, our stories are more interesting to others than to us personally. Second, most people who need Christ are not coming from some type of crazy background. The average guy who needs Jesus goes to work each day, goes to his kids' sports games on weekends, and is committed to his wife. The average woman who needs Christ may be a career woman trying to pay bills or a stay-at-home mom struggling to take care of the kids and feeling like there has to be more to life than washing dishes and cooking dinner. These people may not relate to the story of a recovered alcoholic, gang member, or ex-addict. They may benefit most from a simple story of a simple person who, from the outside, looked like she was living the dream but, on the inside, was lonely and distant from God. Whatever your story, people in your life need to hear it.

Remember and Tell of the Goodness of God

I am writing this to help you walk out your calling as a living epistle to people in your life. You will reach people I will never talk to, and even if I had the opportunity, they might not be open to me like they are open to you. Another reason writing out your story can be powerful is that your story will begin to fill your heart and mind once again. Let's repeat again Luke 6:45: "For the mouth speaks what the heart is full of."

So, when your heart is filled with the memories and realities of the goodness of God, you will want to share your joy in every conversation. When you deliberately write and rehearse your story, you will share it more often.

Action Steps

Read: 2 Corinthians 3:1-6

Reflection: Reflect and/or journal on the idea that you and your life are like a letter written for others to understand, and to tell people about God. How does that make you feel about where you are, and how you want to continue to grow to help others understand God's power in your life?

Action/Conversation:

1. Write out a long, unedited version of your faith journey with Christ.

2. As a bridge to sharing the gospel, perform an act of kindness and then use the conversation to explain how God leads you to do good things.

EPILOGUE

The bottom line is, if a person is a follower of Jesus, he should be focused on the things Jesus was focused on and do the things Jesus did. The goal of *The Twenty-One Laws of Evangelism* is to build your faith to win souls. I call my twenty-one points "laws" because they are facts and principles God has established.

By focusing on scriptures that give us God's point of view on evangelism, our mindset can change. Our faith will grow as we come to see people in light of their need to connect with Christ. We will see others through the lens of God's love. He wants everyone in eternity with Him and wants to give each person abundant life here and now. However, this can only be achieved when a person is in relationship with Christ and being led by the Holy Spirit. And that relationship can only begin after he hears the gospel and has someone (you) explain it to him.

It has been said many times and in many ways that you may be the only Jesus that people ever see. Not that you are Jesus, but that He is in you and you must look and act like Him. Many people are searching for God but have no one to help them. They are waiting for you. Don't wait for a formal ministry title or position. The only title you need is "child of God." If you have put your faith in Jesus for your salvation, then you qualify to be an ambassador.

The same Holy Spirit that raised Jesus Christ from the dead lives in you. This same Holy Spirit will bring new life to those with whom you share the gospel. Be encouraged; God wants to use you to win your friends, family, and anyone you meet. It is His will and now you have twenty-one laws, taken from God's Word, to help you.

I pray God uses you mightily to win one soul at a time. May heaven be full and hell be empty. Thank you for taking the time to read *The Twenty-One Laws of Evangelism* and for sharing Christ with many in the days ahead.

END NOTES

1   http://www.goodreads.com/quotes/74181-if-sinners-be-damned-at-least-let-them-leap-to

2   www.physicsclassroom.com/class/1DKin/Lesson-5/Acceleration-of-Gravity

3   http://www.goodreads.com/quotes/45537-let-my-heart-be-broken-by-the-things-that-break

4   http://www.goodreads.com/quotes/22155-i-like-your-christ-i-do-not-like-your-christians

5   http://www.goodreads.com/quotes/154682-have-you-no-wish-for-others-to-be-saved-then

6   **Redmond, Jack.** *Let Your Voice Be Heard: Transforming from Church Goer to Active Soul Winner.* NY, NY: Morgan James Publishing, 2016. p. 99-101

7   http://www.pewforum.org/religious-landscape-study/

8   http://www.dictionary.com/browse/reconcile?s=t

9   http://diplomacy.state.gov/discoverdiplomacy/diplomacy101/people/170341.htm

10   http://www.dictionary.com/browse/reconciliation?s=t

11   **Oswald, Roy, R. and Speed B. Leas.** *The Inviting Church.* Washington DC: Alban Institute, 1987. p. 44

12   **Redmond,** 99-101

SHARING YOUR STORY OUTLINE

1. **Sharing Your Story**

    a) Followers of Christ: Do what He did (Jn. 14:12). He came to seek the lost (Lk. 19:10).

    b) This means every follower of Jesus is called to speak on His behalf (2 Cor. 5:20).

    c) One of the easiest ways to effectively share the gospel is to share the story of how you became a follower of Jesus.

    d) When it comes to helping people connect with Jesus, we should look at it as a *process*, not just an event.

REDMOND SCALE OF THE EVANGELISM JOURNEY[12]

The Redmond Scale describes general categories and possible feelings of people who are disconnected from Jesus. The role of the Christ follower is to walk with people on a journey to Jesus. On that journey, people must overcome or resolve different feelings, gain knowledge, correct wrong knowledge, and possibly overcome negative religious experiences. Though salvation happens in a moment, there is most often a process to get to that point.

7	Anti-God	Atheistic with a strong anti-religious or anti-God philosophy and negative emotions towards God or religion. Feel that belief in God or religion is a bad thing that represents foolishness or deception.

6	Atheistic	Belief that God is not real, but with little or no strong emotional bias against God or religion. View God as a fairytale or creation of man.
5	Disinterested	Religion or God is not part of regular life. They are fine if others want to be religious, but they have no interest in God or religion. May have a vague belief in God but no real understanding of commitment to God or religion.
4	Religious or "Spiritual"	Committed to a religion, spirituality, or philosophy other than Christ. This can include religions such as Judaism, Islam, and Hinduism, and philosophies such as Buddhism, New Age, or Humanism. In a nutshell, they may be religious, "spiritual," or "believe in God," but they are purposely not committed to Christ with considerable barriers to Christ.
3	Curious	Can be from any background but have come to a place where they are investigating the claims of Christ and the Bible as a possibility in their life and as something special and different than their current understanding of God and religion. Starting to understand that sin is real and a problem in their life.
2	Want Relationship	Relationship now takes priority over religion, philosophy, and good works. They are disentangling from past emotional, situational, and intellectual thought processes and replacing them with Biblical thoughts and desires. Understand sin is a personal problem separating them from God.
1	Ready for Christ	Have investigated the claims of Christ and are ready to embrace them. They have worked through barrier questions and rejected other spiritual and philosophical options. Now understand they are a sinner in need of a Savior.
0	Salvation/ New Life	True repentance of sin takes place, faith is placed in Jesus, and the work of the cross and a commitment to follow Jesus takes place. This is the starting line of a personal relationship with Jesus and the Christian life.

2. **Keys to Effectively Sharing Your Story**

    a)   Speak conversationally: Don't preach. Talk in the same manner you normally do.

    b)   Help the listener feel: Tell your story in such a way the listener will feel as if he was there when your life was changed.

    c)   Understand that your listener is making the decision of a lifetime; it may take time for him to feel sure.

    d)   If you are able to help someone move closer to salvation, that is success.

    e)   Be confident that, over time, God will continue to draw the listener to Him.

3. **Write Your Story**

    1.   How did you come to know Christ?

        _____

        _____

        _____

        _____

    2.   What were the major turning points?

        _____

        _____

        _____

        _____

3. What was your mental and emotional state at that time in your life?

    _____

    _____

    _____

    _____

4. Describe your "aha" moment—the moment you knew you wanted to know and serve Jesus.

    _____

    _____

    _____

    _____

5. What happened inside your heart after you received Christ? How did your perspective on life change?

    _____

    _____

    _____

    _____

Bridging the Gap*

Key points and scriptures in sharing the gospel:

a) God wants an eternal relationship with you (Jn. 3:16, Eph. 1:17, Col. 1:16).

b) Our sinful choices have broken the relationship (Rom. 3:23, 6:23a; Isa. 59:2).

c) Jesus is the bridge back to this relationship (Jn. 5:24, 14:6; Rom. 6:23b).

d)   We must choose to be loyal to this relationship (Jn. 1:12; 15:13-14).

* By understanding and knowing these scriptures and principles, you can weave these truths into your conversation as you share how they worked in your life and can work in the life of the person you are sharing with.

Next Steps

Write out a long version of your story. Then condense it and share it with others. Continue to clarify your story until you can share it in three to five minutes in a relaxed, conversational manner.

Previous Books Written

Transformed
The 7 Pillars of a Legacy Minded Man
with Joe Pellegrino
www.legacymindedmen.org

Let Your Voice Be Heard
Transforming from Church Goer to Active Soul Winner

God Belongs in My City
with Daniel Sanabria
www.GodBelongsinMyCity.org

Infusion
Receive. Grow. Give it Away…

Wounded Heart
Overcoming Life's Pain and Disappointments

People Matter to God

To connect with Jack Redmond, please to to:
www.jackredmond.org

ABOUT THE AUTHOR

Jack's greatest passion is to help others live out their God given purpose by walking in God's power in greater ways. He is an author, speaker, certified life coach, consultant and local church pastor. He does this on local, regional and international levels as Founder and President of Jack Redmond Ministries.

His graduate work includes an M.Div. in Church and Ministry with a specialization in Leadership Development from Regent University and an M.Ed. in Applied Physiology from Columbia University. He is also a certified life coach working with both individuals and small groups. Prior to ministry, his career was in teaching in both in public schools and university level, as well as working as an Athletic Trainer at the high school, college and professional levels.

Jack has been a member of Christ Church in New Jersey for over 20 years, beginning in 1997. He has also served on its staff since July 2000. During this time, he and his team grew their Youth Ministry from 50 to over 850 teens. Transitioning to Church Mobilization Pastor in 2014, he has developed and led Christ Church's evangelism, assimilation and discipleship systems which have resulted in growth from 7000 to 8700 members by 2017.

He has trained thousands on leadership development, church growth and developing systems for both the local church and at regional and national conferences. Jack has also partnered with many churches and ministries to develop training materials for leadership growth, evangelism, prayer, men's ministry and youth ministry.

Jack and his wife Antoinette live in NJ with their four daughters.

ABOUT JACK REDMOND MINISTRIES

Jack Redmond Ministries exists to:
Mobilize People to Purpose and Power

Jack Redmond Ministries works to help people reach their full potential and purpose as individuals, and in their organizations and churches. This is done through live teachings and trainings, online resources, books and training manuals.

Each person has been created for relationship with God and ministry towards others. Christianity is a 24/7 mindset of being ready to be used by God both in our daily lives and intentional ministry efforts. As people walk in God's Power, they can achieve God's purposes in their personal lives and in serving others.

From one on one interactions, church services to regional, national and international conferences, Jack Redmond seeks to help people continually move to the next level of their individual and organizational purpose.

To request Jack Redmond for coaching, consultation, speaking or trainings, go to **www.jackredmond.org**

96709702R00107

Made in the USA
Columbia, SC
03 June 2018